Mediterranean Diet

The Complete Mediterranean Diet For Beginners With 101 Heart Healthy Recipes

By Susan T. Williams

Table of Contents

Introduction vii

Chapter 1: What exactly is the Mediterranean Diet? 1

Chapter 2: Why should you consider the Mediterranean Diet? 9

Chapter 3: How to use the Mediterranean Diet to lose weight? 11

Chapter 4: Recipes for Breakfast 13

    Dates with Nutty Couscous 13

    Mediterranean Scrambled Eggs with Vegetables 14

    Bell Pepper Tagine 15

    Cheese and Zucchini Frittata 16

    Yogurt with Cinnamon Honey Caramelized Figs 16

    Fava Beans Stew with Warm Pita Bread 17

    Cheesy Avocado Toast 18

    Greek pancakes with fruits and nuts 19

    Herbed Ricotta Pita with Olives 19

    Berry Greek Yogurt with Nuts 20

    Tangy Oatmeal with Italian Herbs 21

Chapter 5: Recipes for Lunch 23

    Mediterranean Grilled Sardines with Skordalia 23

    Baked Stuffed Tomatoes 24

    Portobello Mushrooms with Mediterranean Mix 25

    Basil Prawn Pasta 25

    Vegetarian Greek Salad with Black-eyed Peas and Orzo 26

    Grilled Prawns with Baby Spinach and Tzatziki 27

    Salmon Sauté with White Beans 28

    Linguine with Basil and Anchovy Tapenade 29

    Salmon and Eggs on a Bed of Lettuce 29

    Mediterranean Potato Salad 30

    Lamb Moussaka 31

Fattoush Salad 32

Mediterranean Moujadara 33

Vegetable Ratatouille Stew 34

Seafood Paella 34

Greek Lentil Soup with Bell Pepper and Feta Cheese 35

Italian Herb Risotto 36

Spaghetti Squash 37

Tunisian Fish Ball Tagine 37

Quick and Easy Tomato Feta Salad 38

Herby Farro Salad 39

Broccoli Rabe with Sun-Dried Tomatoes 40

Grilled Bell Pepper Salad 40

Steamed Salmon with Avocado 41

Pomegranate Farro Tabbouleh Salad 42

Halibut Stew 43

Linguine with Garlicky Shrimp and Green Beans 44

Greek Salad Pita Pockets with Hummus 44

Roasted Vegetables with Balsamic Vinegar 45

Anchovy with Broccoli Rabe 46

Chapter 6: Recipes for Dinner 47

Lemon Garlic Shrimp with Asparagus and Bell Peppers............ 47

Goat Cheese Roasted Vegetables 48

Mixed Seafood Risotto... 49

Eggplant and Tomato Pasta Bake... 50

Seared Salmon with Lemon Basil Risotto 51

Slow Cooker Beef Ragout 52

Grilled Eggplant Salad with Feta and Walnuts........................... 52

Eggplant Parmigiana... 53

Anchovy Puttanesca Pasta 54

Mediterranean Deviled Eggs 55

Greek Paidakia Lamb Chops with Roast Potatoes 55

Souvlaki Kebabs With Veggies.. 56

Shrimp Saganaki... 57

Greek Spanakopita Spinach Pie 58

Table of Contents

Yemista (Veggie Stuffed Tomatoes)..59

Aginares a la Polita (Constantinople Style Artichokes)...........................60

Mila Gemista Me Kima (Beef Stuffed Apples)......................................61

Kotopoulo me bamies (Chicken Stew with Okra)..................................61

Orange, Anchovy and Olive Salad...62

Sardine Salad..63

Tuscan Chicken..64

Skillet Prawns in Feta Cheese...64

Mediterranean Pork with Orzo...65

Greek Pastitsio Baked Pasta...66

Chicken Saltimbocca...66

Testi Kebab Casserole..67

Kolokithakia Gemista (Stuffed Zucchini)..68

Quinoa Tabbouleh..69

Shakshuka Poached Eggs in Tomato Sauce...70

Tunisian Chickpeas and Vegetable Tagine..70

Chapter 7: Recipes for Desserts, Snacks and Beverages..........................73

Desserts...73

Yiaourti Me Meli (Yogurt, Honey and Walnuts)....................................73

Ginger Watermelon Sorbetto..74

Banana Pineapple Gelato..75

Stewed Apricots with Yogurt and Honey..75

Warm Cinnamon Spiced Fresh Oranges with Honey..............................76

Dried figs, dates and almond balls...76

Loukoumades...77

Maltese Cherry Tart..78

Dried Figs Stuffed with Almonds..79

Peaches in Cinnamon Spiced Wine..80

Snacks...81

Warm Cherries topped with Almonds and Cheese.................................81

Chickpea Patties with Tahini Sauce...81

Rosemary and Pepper Marinated Olives with Feta Cheese......................82

Shallow Fried Cheesy Zucchini Balls...83

Baked Sweet Potato Wedges with Cheese and Garlic.............................84

Fresh Mozzarella, Cherry Tomato and Basil Sticks................................85

Moroccan Toasted Almonds with Cilantro 85

Spinach and Feta Cheese Toast 86

Roasted Eggplant Hummus 86

Spiced Chickpea Tidbits... 87

Beverages... 88

Date and almond smoothie.. 88

Orange, Lime and Pineapple Smoothie 88

Pomegranate Lemonade with Ginger Juice... 89

Almond, Cashew and Berry Smoothie 90

Rose and Raspberry Cooler... 90

Fruity Tea Sangria 91

Creamy Fig, Banana and Almond Smoothie 91

Spicy Pomegranate Surprise 92

Ayran (Turkish savory yogurt drink) 93

Healing Grapefruit Juice.. 93

Conclusion... 95

Our Other Books... 97

Introduction

The Mediterranean Diet has evolved naturally and is the result of many centuries of cross-cultural exchange and refinement.

It is not a diet in the strictest sense but rather a natural dietary tradition. It is therefore easier to adapt to because it is wholesome in its approach and contains comparatively fewer restrictions than most other modern diet plans.

Go on a journey to the center of culinary history.

The Mediterranean Diet is among one of the oldest diets known to man. It comes from a region where some of the earliest civilizations in the western world originated, the Greek and the Roman civilizations.

The meaning of the term 'Mediterranean' which comes from Latin can be interpreted as "in between lands" or "in the middle of the earth." This is significant since the Mediterranean Sea is situated where three continents –Africa, Asia and Europe – meet.

Just as the Mediterranean region represents a geographical and cultural crossroad, the Mediterranean Diet is a combination of different culinary traditions. It is important to understand that the Mediterranean Diet represents not just a way of eating but a way of life.

It makes sense therefore to adapt the Mediterranean Diet in a holistic manner by more than just choosing the right kind of food but also by preparing and eating it the way the ancient Greeks and the Romans did.

Needless to say, combining the Mediterranean Diet with an active lifestyle will make it more enjoyable and produce healthier results.

How did the Mediterranean Diet gain popularity?

Awareness about the Mediterranean Diet in America and the rest of the world can be traced to studies conducted in the 1960s by Dr Ancel Keys, an American scientist who was interested in the relationship between diet and health in general and between diet and disease prevention in particular.

He studied the dietary habits of the inhabitants of different countries in order to determine why Americans despite having what was then believed to be a healthy diet were more susceptible to heart diseases than some Europeans.

The findings clearly indicated that the American diet was more similar to the eating habits of the inhabitants of many north European countries. The dietary traditions of these countries predominantly consisted of meat, butter, dairy and animal fats and a comparatively lesser amount of fish, fruits and vegetables.

In sharp contrast, the inhabitants of the Mediterranean region, especially Greece and Italy, including the islands of Crete and Sardinia, consumed fresh fish, fruits and vegetables on a daily basis while eating meat, eggs and dairy products in moderation.

What are the benefits of the Mediterranean Diet?

The Greek and the Italians had remarkable longevity while enjoying great health, and most of them were living completely disease-free lives. Most significant was the near absence of common modern day diseases like asthma, diabetes and cancer, as well as very low incidence of cardiovascular disease and chronic obstructive pulmonary disease.

Dr. Keys' theory was that the people who lived around the region bordering the Mediterranean Sea were healthier mainly because of their diet.

More recent studies have indicated that this diet along with the active yet relaxed and stress-free lifestyle of the area's inhabitants, contributed to improving metabolism, controlling cholesterol and blood sugar levels and preventing the onset of most modern ailments like diabetes and heart disease.

The evidence for the truism, we are what we eat, has never been more pronounced than in the case of the Mediterranean Diet. While there are many studies that establish the healthy attributes of eating like the people in the Mediterranean region, a simpler way to approach things is to just look at the delicious variety of dishes that constitute the Mediterranean Diet.

Lose weight without losing heart.

From bruschetta to paella, from the gazpacho to the anytime snack of falafel, from the irresistible baba ghanoush to the tantalizing tzatziki, the Mediterranean Diet is as much an epicurean delight as it is a healthy diet. It is perhaps the only diet where eating is not associated with guilt or restriction but with pleasure.

If you want to get healthy and lose excess weight, wouldn't you like to enjoy it? Instead of asking you to give up eating food that you enjoy or asking you to eat less, the Mediterranean Diet recommends that you eat abundantly, albeit the right kind of food.

You will rarely see obesity on the islands of Crete and Sardinia, nor will you see any overweight people in Greece, Italy or Turkey.

Though the Mediterranean Diet is not specifically recommended for the purpose of losing weight, there are many research studies that indicate that those who follow the Mediterranean Diet sincerely in combination with moderate physical activity find it easier to lose weight and also keep their weight under control. You can further customize a Mediterranean Diet to lose weight by strictly eliminating the main culprits that contribute to weight gain such as sugar, processed grains, milk and most dairy products as well as all kinds of processed food.

Stay healthy by preventing diseases.

The widespread use of olive oil in the Mediterranean Diet supplies monounsaturated fat to the body, which is known to prevent cardiovascular disease. Eating fruits and vegetables which are rich in antioxidants on a daily basis can contribute to reducing the risk of cancer.

Fish, especially oily fish such as sardines, which are rich in omega-3 polyunsaturated fat, possess excellent anti-inflammatory properties and act as an efficient vasodilator. Eating oily fish once or twice a week as they do in the Mediterranean region will help regulate blood pressure and prevent the onset of asthma, arthritis and diabetes.

For example, the combination of vegetables, olive oil and fish found in a Greek salad creates a potent nutritional concoction that helps prevent disease and provides the essential nourishment for an active and healthy lifestyle. Leafy green vegetables such as spinach, lettuce and cabbage provide plenty of vitamin C, potassium, calcium and fiber, along with carotenoids and cancer-fighting indoles.

Feast for life.

Every ingredient in the Mediterranean Diet has a healthy story to tell. Chickpeas are a great source of protein as well as calcium and iron. By eating chickpeas on a regular basis, you get a healthy combination of soluble and insoluble fiber, phytates and physterols which help prevent diabetes, colon cancer and heart disease.

The presence of peppers as a staple ingredient in Mediterranean recipes means a regular supply of vitamins A, C and K, fiber, folate and beta carotene. Add the ubiquitous tomato and you have vitamin C and lycopene. All of these in combination have great anti-viral qualities and prevent a range of ailments from macular degeneration and common infections to cancer.

What makes the Mediterranean Diet tasty and enjoyable yet healthy and lean?

Is it the lentil soup or the quinoa salad? Is it the hummus or the tabbouleh?

From preparing a traditional pesto to different types of pasta, from the tahini to the tzatziki, this book presents a plethora of delicious recipes that will keep you healthy and also satisfy your appetite for variety.

101 ways to lose weight and prevent disease

Discover an array of flavors in the 101 Mediterranean Diet recipes presented here. It is the best way to indulge your taste buds without compromising your health. Enjoy your journey towards losing weight and gaining a disease-free healthy lifestyle.

'Cook easily, live happily' seems to be the motto behind the Mediterranean Diet. You will find that the recipes are delightfully easy to prepare and before too long, you will be an expert in adding your own variations. But before we go on to the recipes, let's spend a few minutes to examine the history, benefits and significance of the Mediterranean Diet in today's modern lifestyle.

This will impart you with background knowledge that will help you better appreciate the nutritional benefits of the key ingredients used in the recipes and also enable you to use them to your advantage. Whatever your motivations to try the Mediterranean Diet, whether it is to lose weight or control it, or whether you wish to prevent diseases and live a healthier life, knowing the history and science behind the diet will equip you with a deeper understanding. You will be able to truly appreciate and enjoy every meal.

CHAPTER 1

What exactly is the Mediterranean Diet?

O ne of the conventional ways to define a diet is to define what you are allowed eat. The Mediterranean Diet is more than what you eat but also how, when and with whom you eat. However, we'll come to that later in this chapter. First, we will look at the main food ingredients that make up the Mediterranean Diet.

Fruits

Fruits are an indispensable part of the Mediterranean Diet. They can be included in all your meals but should be the most important part of your breakfast. Eating fruits multiple times a day is encouraged. If you are in the habit of eating a dessert, include a fruit bowl or fruit salad with every meal.

Fruits are a rich source of vitamins, minerals and fiber as well as antioxidants. They also contain phytochemicals that help prevent disease. They are an excellent source of energy but do not have the disadvantage of making you fat like processed food products high in artificial sugar. The fiber content in fruits fills you up so that you feel satiated, thus preventing you from overeating.

It is important that you eat fruits that are fresh and in season. This means you don't have to necessarily eat an apple every day. Instead choose a variety of fruits that are available during that particular season and are locally produced. Include as much variety as possible.

Eat at least 4 to 5 different types of fruit for every serving. Do not forget to include berries such as strawberries, blueberries or raspberries, all of which are rich in antioxidants.

Two important caveats need to be mentioned here. Do not eat canned fruits. Do not substitute fruit juice for fresh fruits.

Canned fruit contain preservatives as well as processed sugar, and eating this will be counter-productive if you are trying to lose weight. Fruit juice, even when you juice it fresh, breaks down the nutritional value of the fruit. Commercially produced fruit juices, on the other hand, are even less nutritious and definitely harmful because they may contain preservatives and processed sugar which will easily make you gain weight.

When you eat fruits that are freshly cut, you consume a lot of fiber which has digestive benefits. Fiber also slows the absorption of the sugar in the fruit. It has been found that while eating fruit lowers the risk of type 2 diabetes, drinking fruit juice can actually increase the risk.

Make eating fruits a daily habit. Start your day with a bowl of fresh fruits, and you will soon notice the difference, not only on the scale but in your overall health.

Vegetables

Remember what your mother or grandmother used to say? Eat your veggies and greens if you want to grow strong. When you follow the Mediterranean Diet, you should include vegetables with every meal.

Eat vegetables for lunch and dinner and possibly, even for breakfast. It is important to have a variety of different vegetables because each one has its unique benefits.

Leafy green vegetables are an excellent source of vitamin, fiber and calcium. Broccoli, cabbage, kale, lettuce, spinach, mustard greens and turnip greens, to name just a few, are some of the green vegetables that can keep you energetic and healthy.

Besides giving you a glowing complexion and combating the visible effects of aging, they also aid in lowering your cholesterol levels and preserving your vision. Leafy green vegetables boost bone health and are also a nutritional powerhouse giving you energy and fulfilling your daily needs for strength and stamina. As Popeye the Sailor says, "I am strong to the finish 'cause I eats me spinach."

Red, green, yellow and orange peppers make a salad look as good as it tastes. They provide essential vitamins, fiber, folate and beta carotene. Red peppers contain lycopene, lutein and zeaxanthin, which are known to provide protection from macular degeneration.

Many a Mediterranean dish would be incomplete without the versatile and ubiquitous tomato. Despite it being used abundantly in salads and sauces, it is interesting to note that the tomato was not always a native of the Mediterranean region, but is believed to have been introduced to Europe by one of the early explorers to the New World, either Cortez or Columbus. These savory and succulent orbs are packed with vitamin C and lycopene and have been known to be instrumental in preventing a host of ailments including cancer.

Virtually all kinds of vegetables can be used in preparing many a Mediterranean dish. You can eat them raw in salads or grilled or steamed. There are dishes you can prepare by stuffing one vegetable with chopped pieces of others, roasting a mixture of vegetables or adding them to fish, seafood or meat.

Asparagus, beans, cauliflower, cucumber, garlic, onion, potato, zucchini and so on are just some of the many vegetables you can use to whip up a delicious Mediterranean breakfast, lunch or dinner.

Last but not least, the eggplant warrants a special mention. This main ingredient in baba ghanoush, a worldwide favorite, is known for its versatility as a crunchy grilled favorite or a light and healthy snack when cut into succulent strips and accompanied by sauces and dips. The eggplant is also not without its nutritional benefits which include providing antiviral protection and preventing cancer.

Needless to say, eat your vegetables fresh and raw, grilled or cooked mildly so that their flavor is enhanced and their nutritional value retained. Eating them in combination with olive oil, either cooked or as a salad dressing, is believed to amplify their nutritional benefits.

Olive Oil

Olives and olive oil are essential ingredients in the Mediterranean Diet. Olive oil can be called the elixir of the Mediterranean Diet and is used in preparing almost every dish. It is used not only for cooking but as an ingredient for marinades, as a salad dressing or just to drizzle over any dish as seasoning or for added flavor.

There is hardly any dispute among medical professionals and health and nutrition experts about olive oil's place as one of the healthiest cooking oils and perhaps even the healthiest source of dietary fat. Rich in monounsaturated fatty acids, olive oil is unanimously acknowledged as being better than other cooking oils or butter, which often contain saturated fats and trans fats.

Traditionally, olive oil has been a cornerstone of the Mediterranean Diet. Through the ages, it has even been venerated as a symbol of health, especially in Greece, where it is believed that in ancient times winners of the Olympic Games were rewarded with jugs of olive oil.

The benefits of olive oil are numerous. It is considered to be one of the main reasons why the inhabitants of the Mediterranean countries enjoy longer life and have minimal risk of heart disease and diabetes. Several research studies indicate that people who regularly consume food fried in olive oil do not face health risks such as heart disease or cholesterol which is normally associated with eating food fried in butter or most other types of oil.

There is also growing evidence that points to the use of extra virgin olive oil as a protectant from Alzheimer's disease, acute pancreatitis and ulcerative colitis. It has been further observed that in addition to the prevention of many types of cancers, olive oil favorably modifies the immune system and strengthens the body's inflammatory response against infection.

Legumes

Chickpeas, fava beans, black-eyed peas and lentils are some of the legumes that are consumed on a daily basis as part of the Mediterranean Diet. Known sometimes as "poor people's meat" for its protein content, they are a nutritionally preferable substitute for meat because, unlike meat, they are cholesterol-free and contain no saturated fat.

They also provide essential protein, fiber, vitamins and minerals such as iron, zinc, magnesium and potassium. One of the main benefits of eating legumes comes from its complex carbohydrate content which make you feel satiated even when you eat smaller portions. This prevents you from consuming unnecessary calories. Eating legumes gives your body energy without adding more pounds to your weight.

Nuts and seeds

Almonds, pistachios, sesame seeds, hazelnuts and walnuts are some of the nuts and seeds that are often found in Mediterranean Diet recipes. Nuts and seeds are rich in dietary fiber and healthy fats.

In other words they are so densely packed with nutritional value, that you should be careful not to consume too much of them.

Fish and seafood

It is no surprise that some of the inhabitants of the Mediterranean region eat fish and seafood with almost every meal. After all, it is easily available and plentiful. Typically as part of the Mediterranean Diet, it is recommended that you consume fish or seafood at least twice a week.

Some of the most favored fish in Mediterranean Diet recipes are anchovies, herring, mackerel and sardines. Of course, other seafood such as prawns, squids and oysters may also be added.

Fish is a healthier alternative to eating meat. Fish is high in proteins and low in fat unlike most other sources of animal protein. Oily fish in particular such as sardines and mackerel are excellent sources of omega-3 fatty acids which are generally known as the good fats.

There are multiple health benefits that omega-3 provides. These include maintaining cardiovascular health, optimizing blood circulation, protecting and improving vision and protecting your skin from the harmful effects of UV radiation.

Eating fish has also been found to contribute towards improving lung function and relieving asthma, providing relief from rheumatoid arthritis and protecting against osteoarthritis, preventing ulcerative colitis and inflammatory bowel disease and preventing depression.

Fish and seafood are rich in essential nutrients: iodine which is good for the thyroid gland; selenium which makes enzymes that provide protection from cancer; zinc and magnesium which contribute to the normal functioning of the immune system and vitamins A and D.

Eating fish is as good for the brain as it is for the heart. It has been found that people who eat fish regularly are less likely to suffer from dementia or memory problems. It has also been known to improve concentration in children and help overcome ADHD (attention deficit hyperactivity disorder).

As far as flavor is concerned, fish and seafood provide a wider variety of choices than meat.

Herbs and spices

The secret to the variety of flavors that you can savor in many a Mediterranean dish comes from the herbs and spices that are liberally used. Most often theses spices can be a substitute for salt. The list of spices and herbs below present a virtual cornucopia of the multiple influences from different culinary cultures surrounding the Mediterranean Sea.

Here are just some of the herbs and spices prevalent in the Mediterranean diet: anise, basil, bay leaves, cardamom, cinnamon, chives, clove, cumin, coriander, fennel, fenugreek, garlic, lavender, mint, nutmeg, oregano, parsley, pepper, rosemary, saffron, sage, tarragon, thyme and special culinary mixtures of choice spices such as za'atar. It makes sense to pay special attention to the herbs and spices used in the Mediterranean Diet because they are often overlooked, especially by those who are new to the cuisine.

The nutritional benefits of spices and herbs range from their rich antioxidant nature to varied medicinal properties from healing to providing protection from many diseases.

Water and wine

This may seem like stating the obvious to many people, but water is an essential part of a Mediterranean meal. Instead of guzzling on a soda or a beer with your meals, start drinking water, and you will soon start seeing a visible difference in your appearance and the number on the scale.

Water plays an essential part in metabolism, in providing nutrition and in getting rid of the toxins and waste that can build up in the body. After all, the human body is composed of about 60% water. There is no denying that you need to drink water.

Wine as consumed in the Mediterranean Diet can contribute to a healthy lifestyle. Red wine in moderation has been known to be beneficial to the heart. The presence of a flavonoid known as resveratrol in red wine is also believed to aid in weight loss by imitating the benefits of exercise and building muscle strength and physical stamina, as well as preventing the development of cancer.

Having the occasional glass of red wine with your Mediterranean meal can be beneficial. Of course, the inhabitants of Greece and Italy, who lived healthy lives, did not drink more than a glass of red wine with their meals. It goes without saying that drinking too many glasses of wine a day can be counter-productive to losing weight or trying to inculcate healthy lifestyle habits.

The Mediterranean Diet is about moderation.

Now that we have looked at the essential ingredients that make up the Mediterranean Diet, let's consider what you can eat in moderation as part of the Mediterranean Diet and what you should completely avoid or eliminate.

Cereals and grains

It's hard to imagine the Mediterranean Diet without pasta, pizza or couscous. Cereals and grains can be a part of every meal provided they are whole grains such as wheat, oats, rice, rye and barley. It is important that you moderate the portions.

The main focus at any meal should be on vegetables, legumes, nuts and seeds as well as fish and seafood. Cereals or grains should be served as an accompaniment. It is an excellent idea to avoid all kinds of refined and processed grain food products if you are trying to lose weight.

Eggs and meat

Typically meat is eaten once a week or even more rarely in a Mediterranean Diet. When included, meat is consumed in smaller portions and always as a side dish or accompaniment and never as the main dish or focus of a meal. All kinds of meat which are a good source of animal protein, such as beef, chicken, duck, lamb, mutton and pork, can be used. Processed meat such as sausages or hot dogs should be avoided at all costs.

Eggs are used for baking, making omelets or frittatas or can be eaten boiled, poached, or fried. Rich in protein, vitamins and minerals, eggs are highly nutritious and also satisfy your appetite with fewer calories. When eaten sensibly, they can enable you to effectively lose weight.

Milk and dairy

Milk and dairy products are not part of the traditional Mediterranean Diet with the exception of yogurt and cheese. There is increasing evidence that links consumption of milk and dairy products to a greater incidence of cancer, diabetes, osteoporosis and cardiovascular disease. These growing health concerns also indicate that the earlier perceived benefit of calcium from dairy may not be true and that calcium many not be as beneficial to the bones as previously thought.

Can anyone follow the Mediterranean Diet?

Naturally, it is correct to assume that the Mediterranean Diet would consist of food ingredients that are available to people who live in that geographical region. The Med Diet, as it is also called, is typically based on the type of food that is consumed in Greece and Italy, two countries on the Mediterranean Sea.

In a stricter sense, the initial Mediterranean Diet was inspired by the culinary traditions and eating habits of the inhabitants of the islands of Crete and Sardinia. However, evolved versions of the Mediterranean Diet include food from Spain, Southern France and even Portugal, which does not really belong to the Mediterranean region.

Broader versions of the Mediterranean Diet includes food from Asian and European countries bordering the Mediterranean Sea such as Cyprus, Malta, Turkey, Syria, Lebanon and Israel. Influences from African countries on the Mediterranean coast—Egypt, Libya, Algeria, Turkey and Morocco—are also evident in some Mediterranean Diet recipes.

Since the Med Diet is based on the dietary traditions of a particular geographical region, it raises the question if anyone living in a different part of the world can effectively adapt the Mediterranean Diet. The answer is yes. What about the availability of the ingredients, you might ask?

Anyone, anywhere, can eat the Mediterranean way.

The Mediterranean Diet is not a strict regime of food but rather a collection or combination of eating habits from around the Mediterranean region.

Its significant characteristics are eating an abundance of fruits and vegetables, the use of olive oil, cheese and yogurt in the preparation of food, eating fish and seafood more than meat and drinking wine in moderation along with meals.

The Mediterranean Diet emphasizes the importance of eating seasonal and locally produced fruits and vegetables, avoiding or eliminating sugar and processed food and reducing the consumption of milk and dairy products as well as meat.

Why is it important to eat seasonal fruits and vegetables that are produced locally? The freshness and availability of the ingredients contribute to your overall success with the Mediterranean diet.

Acquiring most of the ingredients in the Med Diet is relatively easy and in many instances, it may even turn out to be more cost-effective than eating branded and processed foods.

Savor every meal as a social occasion.

In the beginning of this chapter, we mentioned that food is but one aspect of the Mediterranean Diet. What you eat is as important as when and how you eat it.

Eating your meals on time, whether breakfast, lunch or dinner, is important, and skipping meals is not advisable. Every meal is enjoyed by sitting down and devoting your time and attention to it. The Italians or the Greeks obviously did not gobble a meal while watching TV or distractedly stuffing themselves while texting on the phone.

Meals are also social occasions and not something to be consumed on the go or while working. When you eat with other people, it provides an opportunity to pause and enjoy every bite or morsel you take in. When you eat in the company of others, you also tend to eat slowly and leisurely rather than in a rush. This is beneficial because you eat only as much as you need to, and you are much better able to recognize your body's signals to that your hunger is satiated.

Understanding that the Mediterranean Diet is not just about food but also about making a lifestyle change is important to effectively adapting the eating habits of the Mediterranean region. These habits have contributed to the healthy, disease-free, longer living advantages that the people inhabiting the Mediterranean region have enjoyed for centuries.

CHAPTER 2

Why should you consider the Mediterranean Diet?

Studies show that some of the healthiest and happiest people on earth live in Japan, Italy and Greece. More specifically, the number of people who lead healthy lives for more than 100 years is significantly large among the inhabitants of the islands of Okinawa in Japan, Crete in Greece and Sardinia in Italy.

While genetic and lifestyle factors may contribute to the longer life of the inhabitants, the significance of the common characteristics in their diets cannot be ignored. Just like the Greeks and the Italians, the Okinawans also eat lots of fresh fruits and vegetables as well as whole grains. They also consumed more fish and seafood and a lesser or moderate amount of meat. Their diets are significantly lacking processed sugar, dairy and most modern kinds of processed food.

The Med Diet could be the way to keep disease at bay.

Findings from more recent studies substantiate the theory that the Mediterranean Diet is not only healthier, but that it can even help prevent disease and contribute to losing weight effectively and maintaining an ideal weight.

It has been well established that the incidence of heart disease, cancer, diabetes, hypertension and obesity – some of the most common and serious causes of illness and death in our modern world – is significantly lower among those who eat a Mediterranean Diet.

Is the Mediterranean Diet here to stay?

Diets come and go for many reasons. Either they don't work, or people get tired of them. That's why you have many fads, quick-fixes or so-called crash diets which give you great hopes of instant gratification but fall short on results when it comes to delivering on their promises.

While there are many low-fat diets rich in protein or plant-based diets that claim to reduce cholesterol levels, most of them focus on specific aspects of health at the risk of ignoring others.

The alternative to mixing and matching multiple diets is to find a single diet that has stood the test of time, and the Mediterranean diet singularly satisfies this criteria.

The proof is in its long history.

As a result of following the Mediterranean Diet, people have been living longer, healthier and happier disease-free lives for a long period of time, especially in comparison to many of the other popular diets around. We cannot be absolutely sure whether it is because of the fish or the pasta, the hummus or the olive oil alone that make the Mediterranean Diet so good for you. It may also be the combination of lifestyle factors of those living in the region.

However, it has been well established from many studies that eating a Mediterranean Diet along with positive and long-term lifestyle changes can help you lose weight more efficiently and fast track your journey towards achieving your ideal weight.

In other words, by adapting an active, low-stress lifestyle, you can be sure that the weight you lose by eating a Mediterranean Diet will not return, provided you continue to follow the diet. Also, we know that the Mediterranean Diet has also been found to help prevent the onset of cardiovascular disease, cancer, diabetes, hypertension or obesity as a person grows older.

CHAPTER 3

How to use the Mediterranean Diet to lose weight?

Since there are few restrictions in the Mediterranean Diet, the key to using it to lose weight is to reduce the intake of high-energy food ingredients. Strictly eliminating all food containing processed sugar such as ice creams, cakes or cookies, as well as avoiding processed grain products, processed meat, milk and dairy products other than cheese and yogurt will enable you to lose weight efficiently and also fast track your journey towards your ideal weight.

Eating fruits and vegetables on a daily basis, a varied portion of fish and seafood at least once a week, using olive oil as salad dressing or for cooking, and eating only food made from whole grains will make you feel not only satiated but also provide you enough nourishment to lead an active and healthy lifestyle.

Eat like an Olympian.

It is perhaps not a coincidence that the Olympic Games originated in Greece. This celebration of athleticism, sports, speed and strength is symbolic of how much importance was attributed to health. From ancient times, the value of nutrition in promoting health and longevity was not lost among the inhabitants of Greece, Italy and the other countries surrounding the Mediterranean Sea.

It comes as no surprise therefore that the inhabitants of the Mediterranean region consumed more locally grown produce, which essentially consisted of fruits, vegetables, nuts and a lot of fish and seafood. One of the most significant aspects of the Mediterranean Diet is that even in modern times almost all the food that they consume is from within the region and not commercially processed or produced or imported.

One of the main advantages of the Mediterranean Diet is that you can easily prepare and enjoy a variety of great tasting meals. Simply speaking, the Mediterranean Diet starts with healthy ingredients and continues with a healthier way of preparing them.

Indulge in food that is fresh and tasty.

Instead of processed food products which may seem more convenient, Mediterranean Diet recommends fresh produce that is readily available at a supermarket, vegetable or fruit shop near you or at your local fish monger. Instead of complicated and quick-cooking methods where we overcook, deep-fry or drastically alter the condition of the ingredients, the Mediterranean Diet recommends a gentler and more refined way of preparing your meals, mostly by poaching, steaming or roasting.

When using faster methods of cooking, we are generally subjecting our food to abuse and destroying its nutritional value as well as its natural flavors. The Mediterranean Diet recognizes the importance of treating food with care and enhancing its flavor and nourishing qualities. The result is that you start liking what you eat while you also benefit from eating it.

Moreover, you can even indulge in a glass of wine at mealtimes. There are hardly any restrictions.

Losing weight can be easy and enjoyable, too.

The only types of food you should completely avoid are sugar-sweetened beverages, processed food containing sugar, processed meat, refined grains and the so-called low-fat or diet processed food products. The best part is you will not even miss them because you can replace them with a variety of tasty fresh food.

While saying no to the likes of soda, candies, ice creams, white bread, margarine and sausages is necessary, you can say yes to moderate amounts of red wine, tea, coffee, eggs and meat.

Eat rice, whole grain pasta and couscous on a regular basis with an abundance of fresh fruits, vegetables, fish and seafood. The good thing about the Med Diet is that it has very few restrictions and instead introduces or replaces the unhealthy items in your diet with not just healthier but tastier ones.

CHAPTER 4

Recipes for Breakfast

Begin your day with a hearty breakfast the way the people of the Mediterranean do. Breakfast is the most important meal of the day and besides a generous bowl of fresh cut fruits, here are 10 exciting ways to gain energy which can also help you lose weight along the way. Indulge while eating healthy.

Dates with Nutty Couscous

Do you crave a filling, warm breakfast on a brisk morning? This breakfast dish is loaded with the goodness of dates, without being sickeningly sweet and is a super way to kick-start your day.

Rich in antioxidants, dietary fiber and the essential minerals potassium and magnesium, dates are also an excellent source of iron. Iron is a component of the hemoglobin inside the red blood cells which determines the oxygen-carrying capacity of blood. Dates contain tannins, which are flavonoid polyphenolic antioxidants that have anti-infective, anti-inflammatory and anti-hemorrhagic properties.

Serves 4

Ingredients:

1½ cups couscous
1½ cups water
¼ cup sugar
1 tablespoon unsalted butter
1/3 cup chopped dates

1 cup chopped mixed nuts like walnuts, pistachios, blanched almonds, hazelnuts and pine nuts
1 cup milk, hot

Method:

1. In a large, heavy saucepan, bring water, sugar and butter to boil, stirring to dissolve the sugar.
2. Pour this mixture over couscous that is placed in a different bowl. Stir until it has blended.
3. Cover the bowl and let it stand for five to ten minutes.

4. Now fluff with a fork to separate grains and mix in the nuts and dates into the couscous.
5. Transfer the couscous to a baking dish and allow it cool. Cover the dish with foil.
6. Preheat oven to 350°F and bake the couscous for about 20 minutes.
7. Serve in bowls, with some hot milk and additional sugar on the side.

Mediterranean Scrambled Eggs with Vegetables

Eggs are a great way to start the day. This Mediterranean scrambled eggs recipe combines vegetables, olives and cheese to give you the necessary energy boost in the morning.

Getting enough protein to start the day can help you lose weight. Eggs are protein-packed and also contain amino acids to help the body process the protein easily. With a hearty healthy breakfast of eggs, you are less likely to feel hungry before lunch and thereby snack on something unhealthy. There's enough evidence to indicate olive oil aids in weight loss. It has also been found that the combination of olive oil with veggies enables the body to easily absorb the nutritional value of vegetables such as carotenoid and other antioxidants.

Serves 4

Ingredients:

6 eggs
4 potatoes, sliced thin
1 red bell pepper, diced
8 black olives, pitted and chopped
¼ cup fresh parsley, chopped

¼ cup Ricotta cheese
2 teaspoons olive oil
4 teaspoons extra-virgin olive oil
Salt and pepper to taste
4 slices wholegrain bread

Method:

1. Heat the olive oil in a large skillet. Add the sliced potatoes and sauté until golden brown.
2. Add the diced bell pepper and chopped olives and cook lightly for 2-3 minutes.
3. Pour eggs into a bowl and add chopped parsley and cheese. Whisk the mixture to get an even texture.
4. Pour the mixture into the skillet over the potatoes and stir lightly. Cook till the mixture is firm or until desired consistency is reached. Add salt and pepper to taste.
5. Serve with wholegrain bread slices lightly brushed with extra-virgin olive oil.

Bell Pepper Tagine

Filling up on vegetables for breakfast will fuel you up with enough energy and more to spare. Grilling the vegetables enhances its high-fiber content and the addition of olive oil enhances its nutritional value. Losing weight doesn't mean eating bland food and this Moroccan-inspired spicy stew proves it.

Bell peppers in this healthy stew impart more than just a crunchy flavor to your breakfast. They are low in calories and yet they fulfill your daily need for vitamins A and C, boosting your immune system, aiding in cell regeneration and also boosting the look and feel of your skin and hair. Capsaicin is found in bell peppers and is known to reduce cholesterol, prevent diabetes and ease inflammation.

Serves 4

Ingredients:

1 onion, cut into 4 wedges

2 red bell peppers, cut into large pieces

1 green bell pepper, cut into large slices

¼ cup green olives, pitted and sliced

¾ cup chopped onion

2 garlic cloves, minced

1 teaspoon cumin powder

1/2 teaspoon black pepper, freshly ground

1/2 teaspoon fennel seeds

1/2 teaspoon cinnamon, crushed

6 potatoes, cut into wedges

2 tomatoes, diced

1 teaspoon olive oil

¼ cup walnuts

¼ cup water

Salt to taste

Method:

1. Place onion wedges and the red and green bell pepper pieces into a bowl, and pour ½ teaspoon olive oil over the mixture. Add salt to taste.
2. Heat ½ teaspoon olive oil in a large skillet. Add the chopped onion and garlic and sauté for 3 minutes. Add the spices—cumin, black pepper, fennel, cinnamon—and sauté for a minute. Add salt and water followed by the tomatoes, potatoes and olives. Cover and let simmer till the potatoes are cooked tender.
3. Grill the onion wedges and red and green bell pepper pieces for 10 minutes. Add the grilled vegetables to the stew. Sprinkle with walnuts.

Cheese and Zucchini Frittata

Also known as the Italian omelet, it is one of the tastiest ways to eat vegetables. This frittata will energize you with a high-protein, low calorie breakfast to fast track your weight loss journey.

The combination of eggs, zucchini and cheese makes this frittata a highly nutritious yet light breakfast. Low in calories, zucchinis contain no saturated fat or cholesterol and provide dietary fiber that enhances metabolism. Cheese provides essential nutrients such as calcium, protein, phosphorus, zinc, vitamin A and B12. The protein-rich egg content adds to the energy quotient of this meal.

Serves 6

Ingredients:

8 eggs

1 cup chopped onions

2 cloves garlic, minced

2 zucchinis, sliced

3 tablespoons olive oil

½ cup feta cheese, crumbled

½ cup bell pepper, chopped

½ cup black olives, pitted and sliced

¼ cup fresh basil

1/3 teaspoon black pepper, freshly ground

2 tablespoons finely shredded parmesan cheese

Salt to taste

Method:

1. Preheat oven to 350°F. In a large ovenproof skillet, pour 2 tablespoons of olive oil and cook onion and garlic till onion is tender. Add the zucchinis and cook for 10 minutes.
2. Pour eggs in a bowl and beat to an even texture. Add feta cheese, chopped bell pepper, olives, basil and black pepper powder along with salt.
3. Pour the egg mixture over the onion in the skillet, and cook over medium heat. While the mixture is setting, run a spatula along the edges of the skillet to lift the egg mixture and let the uncooked parts flow under. Cook till the mixture is firm.
4. Your frittata is ready to serve. Cut it into 6 wedges like a pizza. Sprinkle parmesan cheese and basil leaves.

Yogurt with Cinnamon Honey Caramelized Figs

Figs trees are native to the Middle East and Mediterranean. The Greeks held them in such high regard that they created laws to prevent their export at one time. With the pleasant chewiness in the flesh of the figs and the crunch from the fig seeds and the pistachios, you will have a delicious, and gorgeous looking breakfast.

Figs have a high content of natural sugars, minerals like magnesium, calcium, iron, potassium and copper as well as soluble fiber and are a good source of antioxidant vitamins A, E and K.

Serves 2

Ingredients:

4 ounces fresh figs, halved

1 cup plain low-fat Greek yogurt

2 tablespoons honey

A pinch of ground cinnamon

¼ cup pistachios, chopped

Method:

1. Heat a small pan over medium-high heat and spoon in the honey.
2. When the honey is hot, place the figs with cut sides down into the pan. Move around the pan. Cook until the honey caramelizes, and the figs have become soft.
3. Serve over yogurt. Sprinkle cinnamon and pistachios. Like your breakfast sweeter? Drizzle more honey.

Fava Beans Stew with Warm Pita Bread

This hearty breakfast stew is made with fava beans, very high in protein and dietary fiber.

Fava beans are a good source of vitamin B1 and thiamin, which is important for proper functioning of the nervous system. Fava beans also contain iron, an essential component of a protein responsible for transportation of oxygen in the bloodstream. They also offer cardiovascular benefits and aid in weight management.

Serves 4

Ingredients:

2 15-oz can fava beans, undrained

2 tablespoons olive oil

1 large onion, chopped

1 large tomato, chopped

2 cloves garlic, peeled and crushed

1 teaspoon cumin, ground

¼ cup chopped fresh parsley

¼ cup fresh lemon juice

Crushed red pepper flakes, to taste

4 whole-grain pita bread pockets

Salt and pepper to taste

Method:

1. In a large skillet, heat the olive oil over medium-high heat and when hot, add the onion, garlic and tomato. Sauté until soft.
2. Add the fava beans with the liquid, and bring to a boil.
3. Bring the heat down to medium and add the parsley, cumin, and lemon juice. Season with crushed red pepper flakes and salt and pepper to taste. Cook for two-three minutes on medium-heat. Drizzle with more olive oil, and sprinkle with parsley before serving.
4. Heat the pita bread on a skillet over medium-low heat, and serve it with the fava bean stew on the side.

Cheesy Avocado Toast

This quick and easy breakfast toast is a filling little dish that's full of healthy fats and protein which will help keep you going and power you through your morning.

The healthy fats, i.e. the monounsaturated fatty acids, found in avocados help to keep your skin smooth, energize you and provide essential fatty-acids. Avocados also contain nutrients like potassium, vitamins C, K and B6 that your body needs to build muscle and repair tissues, improve the immune system and to give you healthy skin and hair.

Serves 2

Ingredients:

2 small ripe avocados, peeled with seed removed
¾ cup soft feta, crumbled
2 tablespoons fresh mint, plus extra to garnish, chopped

1 tablespoon fresh lemon juice
4 slices rye bread
2 eggs, boiled and quartered into wedges
Salt and pepper to taste

Method:

1. In a medium-sized bowl, roughly mash the avocado with a fork. Add lemon juice and mint, and mash until evenly mixed. Season to taste with salt and freshly ground black pepper.
2. Toast the rye bread until golden. Spoon the avocado paste onto each slice of bread and top with feta. Garnish with extra mint and serve with some hardboiled egg wedges.

Greek pancakes with fruits and nuts

Enjoy a healthy breakfast which offers you the benefit of whole grains and is topped with fresh fruit, toasted nuts and Greek yogurt for extra tang and crunch.

This pancake recipe includes flax seeds which provide excellent health benefits, since they contain essential fatty acids (EFAs), most notably omega-3. Omega-3 can reduce the risk of cardiovascular disease and high blood pressure. This seed of the flax plant, which is native to the Mediterranean and Indian regions, is also known to reduce levels of LDL, or "bad" cholesterol. Since they are high in fiber, they help cure digestive tract problems and lower blood pressure and cholesterol levels.

Serves 4

Ingredients:

½ cup whole wheat flour
1 cup old-fashioned oats
2 tablespoons flax seeds
1 teaspoon baking soda
Salt to taste
2 cups Greek yogurt
2 large eggs

2 tablespoons honey
2 tablespoons canola oil
Fresh fruit like bananas, berries for topping
Handful of toasted walnuts, hazelnuts and almonds, chopped for garnish

Method:

1. Add the flour, oats, flax seeds, baking soda and salt in a blender and process for a minute.
2. Add yogurt, eggs, oil, and honey, and blend until smooth. Allow batter to stand for about 20 minutes or until it thickens.
3. Heat a large non-stick skillet over medium heat, and brush it with oil. Pour ¼ cup of the batter into skillet and spread and cook until golden brown and bubbles form on top. Then, turn over and cook until golden brown.
4. Serve with fresh fruit like bananas, berries, toasted nuts and Greek yogurt.

Herbed Ricotta Pita with Olives

This Italianesque spread has a nice, light feel and taste, and forms a wholesome breakfast in combination with the whole wheat pita bread and tasty black olives.

Black olives supply small amounts of calcium, iron, and vitamin A. They also contain heart-healthy unsaturated fats which can help lower your cholesterol and reduce the risk of developing type 2 diabetes. In addition, these fats can also protect you from high blood pressure and an abnormal heart rate. But remember, they also contain large amounts of sodium so you should limit the quantity you consume at any given time.

Serves 4

Ingredients:

¾ cup ricotta cheese

2 tablespoons chives, finely chopped

1 tablespoon lemon juice, freshly squeezed

1 tablespoon fresh parsley, finely chopped

1 tablespoon Parmesan cheese, grated

2 teaspoons fresh basil, finely chopped

Salt and pepper, to taste

Black olives, pitted and sliced

6 ½-inch whole wheat pita

Method:

1. Combine the ricotta cheese, chives, lemon juice, fresh parsley, Parmesan cheese and basil in a medium-sized bowl, and stir until evenly mixed. Season the ricotta spread to taste with salt and freshly ground black pepper.
2. Fill the pita with the ricotta spread, and sprinkle sliced olives into it.

Berry Greek Yogurt with Nuts

This energy-boosting, low-fat breakfast is big on protein and antioxidants. Antioxidants help your body fight oxidative stress caused by free radicals. This oxidative stress can lead to illness so it is critical to get the proper intake of antioxidants. Greek yogurt is strained to make it thick and creamy, therefore it provides double the protein of regular yogurt with fewer carbohydrates and less added sugar.

Yogurt is rich in probiotics, which are friendly microorganisms like bacteria and yeast, which normally live in the intestines. Friendly gut bacteria means improved digestion, regularity and overall good health.

Serves 2

Ingredients:

6 tablespoons chopped nuts like walnuts and almonds

2 tablespoons pine nuts

2 bananas, sliced

1-2 handfuls berries

2 cups Greek yogurt

Method:

1. Mix the all the nuts together.

2. Separately, mix the sliced banana and berries.
3. Layer ingredients in a bowl with Greek yogurt and enjoy.

Tangy Oatmeal with Italian Herbs

Bring out the sunny Mediterranean in a humble bowl of oatmeal by adding the rich, tangy flavors of sun-dried tomatoes, olives and feta cheese.

Traditionally made with sheep or goat's milk by the Greek, feta cheese is lower in fat and calories than most cheeses. It also contains vitamin B, which helps metabolize food and aids in the production of red blood cells. Feta cheese also contains calcium, which helps prevent loss of bone density.

Serves 2

Ingredients:

1 cup oats
2 cups vegetable stock
1 pinch dried oregano
Salt and pepper to taste
2 tablespoon olive oil

1 clove garlic, minced
½ cup olives, sliced
½ cup sun-dried tomatoes, chopped
½ cup crumbled feta cheese

Method:

1. In a saucepan, combine oatmeal, vegetable stock, oregano and salt and pepper. Cook over medium heat for five minutes. Stir occasionally so that it does not stick to the bottom of the pan.
2. Heat 1 tablespoon olive oil in a pan over low heat. Add garlic, olives and sun-dried tomatoes. Sauté until tender.
3. Mix oatmeal with vegetable mixture, add feta and drizzle with remaining oil.

CHAPTER 5

Recipes for Lunch

Though the Mediterranean Diet encourages the moderate consumption of certain foods such as meat, it allows you to indulge in plenty of vegetables, fish, legumes and nuts. You will find so much variety and nutrition in the following lunch recipes that you will hardly miss meat.

These recipes include ingredients like vegetables rich in fiber and antioxidants; olive oil, olives and nuts high in monounsaturated fats and protein rich fish. You will find it easy to remain energized and healthy while staying slim and trim at the same time.

Mediterranean Grilled Sardines with Skordalia

Combine the fishing tradition of Greece with skordalia (Greek mashed potatoes), and you have a sumptuous yet healthy meal. Almost as popular as hummus, skordalia is another traditional Greek dip made from mashed potatoes. It is spiked with garlic and lemon and a generous amount of olive oil.

Sardines are arguably the most nutritious fish. Rich in omega-3 fatty acids, calcium, iron and potassium, not to mention protein, they are surprising low in calories. The healthy unsaturated fat in sardines helps regulate cholesterol levels and reduce inflammation, thereby reducing the risk of heart disease, cancer and arthritis. The vitamin b12 in sardines stimulates red blood cell production.

Serves 4

Ingredients:

1 pound potatoes, peeled and chopped
8 garlic cloves
¼ cup yogurt
4 tablespoons olive oil
1 lemon

½ teaspoon thyme, chopped
1 pound fresh sardines
1 pound zucchini, sliced
1 red bell pepper, diced
1 onion, sliced

Method:

1. Boil the chopped potatoes in a large covered saucepan. Add garlic and cook for about 15 minutes till the potatoes are tender. Drain water from potatoes and garlic and save the liquid in a bowl.
2. Add yogurt and 2 tablespoons of olive oil to the liquid drained from the potatoes. Squeeze the lemon, and stir until the texture is smooth and even. Add salt to taste to the potatoes and mash them to get an even consistency.
3. Preheat grill pan over medium heat and place the sardines on top. Drizzle 1 teaspoon of olive oil over the fish and sprinkle the chopped thyme. Cook fish for less than a minute or two on both sides.
4. Pour 1 tablespoon olive oil in a pan and cook the bell pepper, zucchini and onions until tender.
5. Serve vegetables and grilled fish along with the lemony-garlic skordalia dip.

Baked Stuffed Tomatoes

Though most Mediterranean Diet meals are typically light, if you are feeling like having something especially light, then this tasty tomato based vegetarian meal is exactly what you need.

Tomatoes are good for the heart, bones, kidneys and eyes. The lycopene in tomatoes are known to help prevent diseases such as cancer. They are also rich in antioxidants, beta-carotene and vitamins which regulate cholesterol levels and maintain blood sugar levels. A sulfur compound called allicin in garlic is known to have potent medicinal properties which can provide protection from the common cold as well as reducing the risk of Alzheimer's disease and dementia.

Serves 2

Ingredients:

2 tomatoes

½ cup garlic, minced

¼ cup feta cheese, crumbled

¼ cup black olives, pitted and sliced

2 tablespoons extra virgin olive oil

2 tablespoon basil, chopped

Method:

1. Preheat oven to 350° F.
2. Cut the tomatoes in half horizontally or crosswise. Carefully scoop out the pulp and seeds into a bowl. Keep the tomato shells aside.
3. Add minced garlic, crumbled cheese, olive oil and basil to the tomato pulp and mix well to get a thick even paste. Spoon the paste into the hollowed out tomato shells.
4. Place stuffed tomatoes on a baking sheet, and bake for 10 minutes.

Portobello Mushrooms with Mediterranean Mix

Quick and easy to make, this mushroom based dish packs enough protein and fiber to fill you up while being low on calories at the same time.

Mushrooms have been found to possess near miraculous medicinal properties while providing plenty of protein. A great substitute for meat, they have been known to contribute effectively to any weight loss plan. They also contain long chain polysaccharides which boost the immune system.

Serves 4

Ingredients:

4 large Portobello mushrooms

¼ cup onion, finely chopped

¼ cup celery, finely chopped

¼ cup carrot, finely chopped

¼ cup green bell pepper, finely chopped

¼ cup red bell pepper, finely chopped

2 garlic cloves, finely chopped

3 cups French bread, cubed and toasted

½ cup feta cheese, crumbled

3 tablespoons olive oil, divided

4 teaspoons Parmesan cheese, grated

¼ teaspoon black pepper, freshly ground

Method:

1. Remove the stems from the mushrooms, and put aside the caps. Finely chop the stems and add the onions, celery, carrot, green and red bell peppers and garlic.
2. Heat a large skillet over medium heat. Pour in 2 tablespoons of olive oil, and cook the finely chopped mushroom stem and vegetable mixture until tender. Add the French bread cubes, freshly ground pepper and feta cheese and toss gently so that the mixture is evenly distributed.
3. Scoop out gills from the mushroom caps and place the caps stem-side up. Bake the mushroom caps for 15-20 minutes. Spoon the mixture on top of the mushroom caps and serve with the remaining spoonful of olive oil evenly drizzled on top.

Basil Prawn Pasta

Packed with protein, fiber and calcium, this meal has a healthy balance of seafood and vegetables. Indulge in a very sumptuous yet light pasta dish cooked in the traditional Italian way.

Prawns are extremely low in calories compared to chicken or beef and contain less than half the calories of meat. Rich in proteins, vitamin and iron, they help build muscle while contributing to weight loss. They also optimize red blood cell production and the distribution of oxygen within the body.

Serves 4

Ingredients:

1 pound prawns, peeled and deveined

8 ounces wholegrain pasta

3 tomatoes, chopped

2 garlic cloves, minced

2 teaspoons olive oil

¼ cup fresh basil, chopped

1/3 cup black olives, pitted and sliced

¼ cup black pepper, freshly ground

¼ cup feta cheese, crumbled

Method:

1. Cook and drain the pasta.
2. Heat olive oil in a large skillet. Add minced garlic and sauté for less than a minute. Add prawns and sauté for an additional minute. Add chopped tomatoes and basil. Simmer for three minutes, or cook until prawns are tender. Add olives and sprinkle black pepper.
3. Combine cooked shrimp mixture with pasta, and toss gently till even distributed.
4. Sprinkle with feta cheese when you serve.

Vegetarian Greek Salad with Black-eyed Peas and Orzo

The freshness of vegetables mixed with the distinct taste of black-eyed peas and orzo makes this Greek salad a dish your whole family can enjoy. Satisfying amounts of protein and fiber make it a filling midday meal, minus the calories. With dishes like this, you can lose or control your weight effortlessly.

Black-eyed peas are a long-standing Mediterranean staple and are an excellent ingredient to add to any weight loss diet. Their high fiber content aids in the digestive process by boosting metabolism. The components in black-eyed peas also contribute to regulating cholesterol levels.

Serves 4

Ingredients:

½ cup dry black-eyed peas (15 ounce cooked)

¾ cup orzo

1 large tomato, diced

1 cucumber, diced

2 or 3 cups romaine lettuce, coarsely chopped or shredded

½ cup black olives, pitted and sliced

4 to 8 pepperoncini, sliced

1 lemon

1 onion, sliced
2 tablespoons fresh parsley, chopped
1 tablespoon oregano, finely chopped
1 cup feta cheese, crumbled

2 tablespoons red wine vinegar, divided
2 tablespoons extra-virgin olive oil, divided
Salt to taste

Method:

1. Cook orzo, drain and put aside. Cook black-eyed peas, drain and put aside.
2. In a bowl, toss together the diced tomatoes and cucumber, sliced onions, olives, shredded romaine lettuce and pepperoncini. Cut and squeeze lemon juice over the vegetables. Sprinkle the parsley and oregano. Pour 1 spoon each of the red wine vinegar and extra virgin olive oil. Toss gently to mix the salad.
3. In a separate bowl, mix the cooked black-eyed peas and orzo along with the feta cheese. Add the remaining red wine vinegar and extra virgin olive oil.
4. Add the mixture of the black-eyed peas, orzo and cheese to the Greek salad. Sprinkle salt and toss gently till evenly distributed.

Grilled Prawns with Baby Spinach and Tzatziki

Light on the stomach and easy to make, this is a versatile lunch meal. Instead of prawns, you can add grilled chicken or lamb and some tomatoes or other vegetables if you want to make it more filling. Almost anything tastes great in combination with tzatziki, the popular Greek dip.

There's growing evidence to support Popeye the Sailor's claim that spinach is the source of strength and stamina. Spinach has been known to boost energy, increase vitality and improve the quality of blood. The phytochemicals present in the leafy green vegetable, called carotenoids, display remarkable anti-inflammatory properties and also reduce the risk of cancer. Since spinach is high in water content, it aids in weight loss while satiating your hunger.

Serves 4

Ingredients:

1 cup Greek yogurt
1 cucumber, diced
3 tablespoons dill, freshly chopped
3 cloves garlic, minced
2 tablespoons shallots, chopped
1 lemon

2 tablespoons aniseed, finely crushed
1 tablespoon pepper, freshly ground
2 tablespoons olive oil, divided
1 pound prawns, peeled and deveined
8 cups baby spinach leaves
¾ cup feta cheese, crumbled

Method:

1. Mix the diced cucumber, dill, garlic and shallots with the Greek yogurt. Add 1 tablespoon each of aniseed and , freshly ground pepper. Cut and squeeze half a lemon over the yogurt mixture. Pour one tablespoon of olive oil. Season tzatziki with salt and refrigerate for an hour or more.

2. Grill prawns on medium heat till tender. Place grilled prawns over the baby spinach leaves in a bowl and squeeze the remaining half lemon. Pour one tablespoon of olive oil and sprinkle one tablespoon of aniseed and feta cheese over the prawns.

3. Spoon the tzatziki generously over prawns and serve.

Salmon Sauté with White Beans

A hearty meal that combines the protein-packed power of salmon with the antioxidant punch of veggies, this meal will fill you up without any worries about calories.

White beans, or cannellini beans, activate alpha-amylase inhibitors which control fat storage in the body. An excellent source of protein and fiber, they are low in calories and therefore an ideal ingredient when you are trying to lose weight. Combined with the omega-3 rich salmon, the dish energizes your body and enriches your blood circulation.

Serves 4

Ingredients:

4 salmon fillets (approximately 6 ounces)
1 onion, chopped
1 tomato, chopped
1 can (15 oz. drained) cannellini beans
or white beans
2 tablespoons olive oil, divided

½ cup black olives, pitted and sliced
2 tablespoons basil, chopped
½ teaspoon pepper
¼ cup parsley, chopped
Salt to taste

Method:

1. Heat 1 tablespoon olive oil in a saucepan. Add chopped onions and sauté for 2 minutes. Add beans, olives and tomato, and cook for 2 minutes, stirring occasionally. Sprinkle basil.

2. Heat remaining 1 tablespoon olive oil in a skillet, and cook salmon fillet for 3 minutes on each side. Sprinkle salt and pepper evenly over the salmon fillets.

3. Serve with salmon placed over white beans mixture. Garnish with parsley.

Linguine with Basil and Anchovy Tapenade

A Provençal favorite meets an Italian staple putting a tasty twist to this Mediterranean meal. Light and filling at the same time, it is easy to prepare and makes for a convenient meal.

Reducing weight, improving skin vitality, strengthening the teeth and flushing out toxins are some of the multiple benefits gained from eating anchovies. Add in the medicinal properties of basil, which acts as a skin cleanser and stress buster, to get a healthy meal that contributes in many wonderful ways to improving overall health.

Serves 4

Ingredients:

1 can anchovy fillets, drained and rinsed or 2 ounces fresh anchovy fillets
3 cloves garlic
1 cup black olives, pitted
1 cup fresh basil leaves, chopped

1 cup fresh parsley, chopped
4 spoons extra virgin olive oil
1 pound linguine pasta
1 cup parmesan cheese, freshly grated

Method:

1. Put anchovy fillets, garlic, olives, basil and parsley in a food processor and whip into a smooth puree. Add 2 tablespoons of extra-virgin olive oil. Your tapenade is ready.
2. Cook the linguine pasta until al dente. Drain and add tapenade, and add the remaining 2 tablespoons of extra virgin olive oil. Sprinkle with parmesan cheese when serving.

Salmon and Eggs on a Bed of Lettuce

Elaborate in the range of flavors yet easy to prepare, this immensely filling meal is rich in proteins and light on calories.

Eggs are highly nutritious. They are rich in protein, vitamin A, B-complex vitamins, phosphorus, folate and selenium. Salmon also provides omega-3 fatty acids. Together they balance the amount of calories you need for a high energy day without making you feel bloated.

Serves 4

Ingredients:

4 eggs
½ pound potatoes, cut into wedges

½ pound green beans
1 tablespoon red wine vinegar

1 lemon

6 tablespoons extra virgin olive oil, divided

2 garlic cloves, minced

½ tablespoon black pepper, freshly ground

1 iceberg lettuce

1 tomato, chopped

1 cup green olives, pitted and sliced

8 ounces salmon fillets

Salt to taste

Method:

1. Boil the eggs, drain, deshell and cut into halves. Set aside.
2. Cook the potato wedges and beans in water and 1 tablespoon of extra virgin olive oil in a saucepan. Pour red wine vinegar over the cooked potatoes and beans. Add tomato, olives, minced garlic and salt to taste.
3. Pour 5 tablespoons of olive oil into a skillet and cook the salmon fillets on both sides till tender. Cut lemon and squeeze the juice over the skillet. Sprinkle pepper and salt to taste.
4. Cut salmon into large pieces. Separate the lettuce leaves. Scoop half an egg, a piece of salmon, a potato wedge, some beans onto a leaf of lettuce and serve.

Mediterranean Potato Salad

Potatoes are a much maligned vegetable because of the unhealthy way most people cook and eat them, as fries or as chips. This traditional Mediterranean salad will bring out the best in a potato—its wholesome taste and nutritional goodness.

Potatoes are rich in vitamin B6, which contributes to cell regeneration, improved brain and nervous system function and improved cardiovascular health. Potatoes are a great source of dietary fiber and provide the necessary sustenance to boost athletic performance and physical activity.

Serves 4

Ingredients:

1 pound potatoes

½ pound green beans, cut into ½-inch long pieces

1 red bell pepper, diced

1 onion, sliced

1 cup black olives, pitted and sliced

¼ cup parsley, chopped

1 tablespoon red wine vinegar

2 tablespoon extra virgin olive oil

1 cup parmesan cheese, freshly grated

Salt to taste

Method:

1. Wash and scrub the potatoes, and place them in a large pot. Pour cold water in until the water level is just above the potatoes. Add salt, cover the pot and cook for 10 to 15 minutes or until the potatoes are tender. Use a knife to pierce the potatoes to check if they are done. Drain the water and set the cooked potatoes aside to cool.

2. In another pot boil water and blanch the beans for 4 to 5 minutes. Drain and set aside.

3. Cut the cooked potatoes into wedges and place in a bowl. Add the blanched beans, sliced onion and diced bell pepper. Add 2 tablespoons of extra virgin olive oil and 1 tablespoon of red wine vinegar. Add the olive slices and the chopped parsley. Add salt to taste. Toss gently so that the ingredients are evenly distributed.

4. Sprinkle with parmesan cheese when serving.

Lamb Moussaka

Moussaka is the Greek and Turkish version of lasagna. An elaborate casserole meal, it's ideal for a weekend lunch. This Greek version of the Moussaka uses béchamel sauce made using almond milk.

Meat when eaten in moderation, as they do in the Mediterranean region, can be healthy. It is rich in iron, zinc and selenium, not to mention a great source of protein which can aid in weight loss. Eating meat twice a month will make it taste even better, and it will become a healthier part of your diet.

Serves 8

Ingredients:

1 pound ground lamb meat
3 eggplants, sliced thick
2 onions, chopped
1 lemon
4 tomatoes, pureed
4 garlic cloves, minced
¼ cup olive oil
1 tablespoon butter
½ teaspoon black pepper, freshly ground
Salt to taste

½ teaspoon cinnamon powder, freshly ground
½ teaspoon nutmeg powder
¼ cup parsley, chopped
½ cup red wine vinegar
2 egg yolks
1 cup almond milk
½ cup chickpea flour
½ cup parmesan cheese, grated

Method:

1. Spread the eggplant slices and sprinkle salt evenly. Set aside for a while so that the eggplant can dry a bit. Heat olive oil in a skillet, and fry the eggplant slices till brown on both sides. Set aside.

2. In a large skillet, add butter and the ground lamb meat along with the garlic and onions. Cut and squeeze the lemon into the skillet. Add salt and pepper. Cook until brown. Sprinkle cinnamon, nutmeg and parsley. Pour tomato puree, red wine vinegar and mix till evenly distributed. Simmer for 20 minutes. Set aside to cool.

3. To make the béchamel sauce, heat olive oil in a saucepan. Add chickpea flour and stir for 5 minutes. Add almond milk and stir for 10 minutes on simmer. Whisk the egg yolks and add to the mixture, stirring to get an even thick texture. Add salt and pepper.

4. Preheat oven at 350°F.

5. Spread half the eggplant slices on a 9x13 inch baking dish. Layer the meat mixture over the eggplant slices. Sprinkle Parmesan cheese over the meat. Layer the remaining half of the eggplant slices and sprinkle the parmesan cheese. Pour the béchamel sauce on top.

6. Bake for 45 minutes at 350°F.

7. Let the moussaka cool for 15 minutes before serving.

Fattoush Salad

This delicious Lebanese dish is quick to make and light on the stomach. The spicy, tangy mix of herbs and vegetables with crispy pita bread pieces are a wholesome and nutritious meal.

Radishes have a lot of fiber and water content which means they aid in digestion and also make you feel satiated without loading you up with unnecessary calories. Besides helping in weight loss, they also have multiple medicinal properties. They are a natural diuretic, aiding in the production of urine and flushing out toxins. They are also rich in anthocyanin, a type of flavonoid that is known to reduce the risk of cardiovascular diseases.

Serves 6

Ingredients:

2 loaves pita bread
1 romaine lettuce, chopped
1 cucumber, chopped
5 tomatoes, chopped

5 radishes, thinly sliced
1 lemon
1 cup parsley, chopped
½ cup olive oil

5 green onions, chopped	½ teaspoon cinnamon powder
1 teaspoon sumac (optional)	Salt to taste

Method:

1. Toast pita bread in toaster oven until crisp. Heat 3 tablespoons of olive oil in a large pan. Break the pita bread into small pieces, and fry in oil until brown. Add salt, pepper and sumac. Set aside.
2. In a large bowl, combine the chopped lettuce, cucumber, tomatoes, green onions and sliced radishes. Add the juice of the lemon and the remaining olive oil to the bowl. Sprinkle cinnamon powder and parsley. Toss gently to distribute evenly.
3. Add the pita bread pieces just before serving so that they don't get soggy.

Mediterranean Moujadara

A Mediterranean dish similar to the British kedgeree, the moujadara is a favorite in the Middle Eastern and Arab countries. It is considered a humble yet wholesome meal for the common folk, and can be eaten with grilled meat or on its own.

Among legumes and nuts, lentils have one of the highest amounts of protein. They also contain other healthy nutrients such as fiber, minerals and vitamins but are surprisingly low in calories and have hardly any fat. If you are trying to lose weight or are trying to control your weight, then eating moujadara will help you in your quest.

Serves 4

Ingredients:

1 cup brown or green lentils	1 teaspoon black pepper, freshly ground
1 cup long-grain rice	Salt to taste
4 onions, halved and thinly sliced	Yogurt
1/3 cup olive oil	

Method:

1. Pour olive oil in a large skillet and sauté the onions over low heat until golden brown. Add salt and pepper.
2. Soak the lentils and rice in water overnight. Drain the water. In a large saucepan, pour 3 cups of water, and add the lentils and rice. Cook without covering for 20 minutes or until the rice and lentils are cooked. Drain any excess water. Mix the onions with the rice and lentils. Serve with a generous dollop of yogurt on top or on the side.

Vegetable Ratatouille Stew

There are very few ways to enjoy a healthy mix of fresh vegetables and herbs than the ratatouille. A perfect meal with plenty of nutritional value and an amazing array of flavors, it's filling but not fattening.

Zucchini is a very low calorie vegetable which has high dietary fiber which boosts digestion. It is also a great source of the heart-friendly electrolyte, potassium. Eggplants, the other ingredient in the ratatouille, contain phytonutrients which improve blood circulation and nourish the brain. The stew is a delicious way to benefit from the nutritional value of many vegetables.

Serves 4

Ingredients:

4 tomatoes, diced
2 zucchini, cubed
1 eggplant, sliced
2 red bell peppers, diced
1 onion, diced
4 cloves garlic, minced
½ cup thyme, chopped

½ tablespoon black pepper, freshly ground
A pinch of saffron
2 tablespoon olive oil
3 tablespoon red wine
1 bay leaf
Salt to taste

Method:

1. In a large saucepan, heat olive oil and sauté garlic and onion until brown. Add bay leaf, eggplant slices, tomato and red wine. Cover and simmer for 10 minutes. When eggplant is tender, add zucchini and red bell pepper. Cover and simmer for 10 minutes. Add salt, pepper and saffron.
2. Add parsley just before serving.

Seafood Paella

The flavors of the sea are a favorite component of Mediterranean meals. A combination of mussels and prawns cooked with vegetables and rice, the paella captures the essence of the fabled feasts in Andalusian fishing villages.

Mussels provide plenty of protein along with selenium, an essential mineral. Eating mussels is known to regulate thyroid hormone levels, improve muscle function and optimize sperm production in men. That's why mussels are thought to be an aphrodisiac. They also contain vitamins that nourish vision and skin, improve red blood cell production and boost the immune system.

Serves 4

Ingredients:

1 pound mussels in shells, scrubbed well	2 cloves garlic, minced
1 pound prawns, peeled and deveined	¼ cup thyme, chopped
2 cups long-grain rice	¼ teaspoon black pepper, freshly ground
1 cup green peas	A pinch of saffron
1 tablespoon extra virgin olive oil	4 lemon wedges
1 onion, chopped	Salt to taste
1 red bell pepper, chopped	

Method:

1. In a large covered saucepan, cook rice with 3 cups of water for 1o minutes. Drain excess water and set aside.
2. Pour olive oil in a large skillet and sauté onion, garlic and bell pepper until tender. Add green peas and prawns and cook for 2 minutes. Add rice, saffron, salt and pepper. Place the mussels on the rice evenly spaced. Cover and cook for 5 minutes or until mussel shells open.
3. Sprinkle thyme and garnish with lemon wedges while serving.

Greek Lentil Soup with Bell Pepper and Feta Cheese

Among Mediterranean Diet meals, lentil soup is one of the most traditional and authentic Greek dishes. This all-season, anytime favorite is a great choice for a light lunch.

As one of the most nutritious minerals and sources of protein, dietary fiber and iron, lentils are great for those who wish to eat light, lose weight and stay healthy. They are also rich in potassium, calcium, zinc, niacin and vitamin K.

Serves 4

Ingredients:

1 cup brown lentils	1 lemon
1 onion, diced	½ cup feta cheese, crumbled
1 red bell pepper, diced	½ tablespoon black pepper, freshly
1 tomato, chopped	ground
2 tablespoon olive oil	Salt to taste
¼ cup thyme, chopped	

Method:

1. Cover and cook the lentils in a large saucepan along with 2 cups water for 15 minutes. Set aside.
2. Pour olive oil in a large skillet, and sauté the onions and red bell pepper for 3-4 minutes or until tender. Add tomato and the cooked lentils. Add water as required, and bring to a boil, stirring occasionally.
3. Add thyme, salt and pepper. Cut the lemon and squeeze the juice on top of the lentils. Serve with feta cheese on top or on the side.

Italian Herb Risotto

Simple yet sumptuous in taste and nutritious in content, risotto is a longstanding Italian tradition. Its versatility makes it an ideal accompaniment with fish, seafood, meat or vegetables.

Herbs like basil, mint, parsley, rosemary, sage and thyme do more than add flavor to our food. They have strong medicinal properties and help protect the body from harmful germs and toxins. They have anti-inflammatory properties and contain antioxidants and vitamins which boost the immune system.

Serves 6

Ingredients:

2 cups Arborio rice
1 onion, chopped
2 zucchini, diced
4 ounces baby spinach, chopped
2 ounces mint, sage and rosemary combined, chopped
1 ounce basil, chopped
1 ounce parsley, chopped
1 clove garlic, minced

6 cups chicken stock
2 tablespoon olive oil
½ cup dry white wine
½ tablespoon black pepper, freshly ground
½ cup parmesan cheese, grated
½ cup yogurt
Salt to taste

Method:

1. In a large saucepan, bring the chicken stock to a boil and simmer.
2. Heat olive oil in another saucepan and sauté the onion and garlic till tender. Add rice and stir occasionally until the rice is evenly coated with oil. Remove from heat and add white wine. Return to heat and cook until wine is absorbed by the rice.

3. Add zucchini, cover and cook until tender. Add spinach, mint, sage, rosemary, basil and parsley. Ladle the stock in portions over the rice so that it is absorbed evenly. Add salt and pepper and cook for 20 minutes.

4. Garnish with grated cheese and serve with yogurt on the side.

Spaghetti Squash

This low-calorie, gluten-free meal is something you should have every week if you are trying to lose weight.

So called because when cooked, the flesh of the spaghetti squash resembles strands of spaghetti, this vegetable contains beneficial carbohydrates, fiber, vitamins and minerals. It has few calories and is heart healthy. It's a great side dish when trying to lose weight.

Serves 6

Ingredients:

1 spaghetti squash, about 3 pounds
1 bell pepper, sliced thin
8 black olives, pitted and quartered
2 tablespoon extra virgin olive oil
1 lemon
¾ teaspoon oregano

½ teaspoon honey
3 tablespoon feta cheese
½ tablespoon black pepper, freshly ground
Salt to taste

Method:

1. Pierce the spaghetti squash in several places using a knife. Place it in a glass baking dish and cook in the microwave on high for 15 minutes.

2. Wait for the squash to cool before handling it, about 10 minutes. Cut it in half lengthwise. Scrape and scoop out the seeds and fibers. Use a fork to twist and remove the spaghetti squash flesh. Place the flesh in a large bowl and set aside.

3. Add the bell pepper, olives and feta cheese to the spaghetti squash flesh. Add the extra virgin olive oil and honey. Cut the lemon and squeeze the lemon juice over the mixture. Add salt and pepper. Toss gently so that ingredients are evenly distributed. Sprinkle feta cheese and serve.

Tunisian Fish Ball Tagine

The variety of fish and seafood dishes is one of the reasons why the Mediterranean diet is so popular among epicureans and health conscious people.

Fish is highly nutritious and contains protein, vitamin B12 and omega-3 fatty acids. Eating fish regularly has been known to provide protection from heart disease, regulate blood pressure levels and greatly reduces the risk of cancer and numerous other degenerative diseases such as Alzheimer's.

Serves 6

Ingredients:

1 ½ pounds white fish, such as cod, sole, snapper or bass

2 onions, minced or pureed

4 garlic cloves, minced

2 tablespoons parsley, chopped

2 tablespoons cilantro, chopped

2 teaspoons cumin seeds, toasted and ground

½ teaspoon black pepper, freshly ground

½ teaspoon salt or to taste

1 ½ cups bread crumbs

1 egg

1 cup olive oil (for the sauce)

3 tablespoon olive oil

2 garlic cloves, minced

5 tomatoes, pureed

1 ½ cups fish broth

½ teaspoon black pepper, freshly ground

Salt to taste

Method:

1. Remove bones in the fish, and chop finely. In a bowl or food processor, combine the fish, onion, garlic, parsley, cilantro, cumin powder, pepper, salt and bread crumbs. Add egg and knead until a smooth and even texture is reached.

2. Dip your fingers in cold water and scoop small portions of the fish paste to roll into balls (about 1-inch all around). Fry the fish balls lightly in olive oil in a large sauce pan and set aside.

3. Warm the olive oil in a tagine or shallow earthen pot. Add garlic, tomato puree, fish broth, salt and pepper and bring to boil.

4. Add fish balls to the sauce. Cover and simmer for 15 minutes. Serve with couscous or as a meal on its own.

Quick and Easy Tomato Feta Salad

Would you believe that tomatoes aren't really native to the Mediterranean region? But thanks to Spanish conquistadors bringing them from the Americas—they are now practically indispensable to Mediterranean cuisine whether fresh, made into a paste or canned.

Tomatoes contain a wealth of nutrients and vitamins including vitamin C and lycopene, an antioxidant that protects your heart and may also help prevent some cancers. They are also a good source of magnesium, potassium, manganese, phosphorous and copper.

Serves 2

Ingredients:

4 vine- ripened tomatoes	1 tablespoon olive oil
½ red onion, thinly sliced	1 tablespoon red wine vinegar
4 oz. reduced fat feta cheese	Salt and fresh ground pepper to taste
1 teaspoon dried oregano	12 black olives in brine, pitted and sliced

Method:

1. Slice tomatoes thickly and place in a large bowl. Scatter the red onions over the tomatoes. Spread crumbled feta cheese over the tomatoes.
2. In a small bowl, whisk together olive oil, oregano and vinegar until thoroughly blended and season with salt and pepper to your taste. Drizzle this dressing over tomato salad and top with the sliced olives.

Herby Farro Salad

Farro salad is a very popular lunch time dish in Italy. It is best when simply adorned with herbs and olive oil, garlic and lemon juice.

Farro is a nutritious grain that has is amazingly low on the glycemic index and delivers a boost of energy for a longer period of time. It is also is a rich source of fiber, vitamin B3, vitamin E, zinc and carbohydrates. Recent research also shows that it is higher in antioxidants than other wheat based grains.

Serves 4

Ingredients:

1 cup farro	1 garlic clove, minced
3 cups water	1 ½ tablespoons lemon juice
1 pound tomatoes, seeded and chopped	¼ cup extra virgin olive oil
1 onion chopped	Freshly ground black pepper and
¼ cup fresh chives	salt to taste
¼ cup fresh parsley leaves, finely chopped	

Method:

1. Mix farro with water in a medium saucepan, add salt to taste and bring to a boil over high heat. Reduce the heat and simmer until farro is tender. This may take about 30 minutes. Drain well, and allow it to cool.
2. Add the tomatoes, onion, chives and parsley to the cooked faro. Toss well.

3. Separately, whisk together the olive oil, garlic, lemon juice, salt and pepper and in a medium bowl. Add this to the salad and toss well.

Broccoli Rabe with Sun-Dried Tomatoes

To enjoy being on a Mediterranean Diet is to appreciate dark leafy vegetables, especially rapini, an earthily bitter brassica called *cime di rapa* in Italy or broccoli rabe in the US. It pairs deliciously with bold ingredients like tomatoes, anchovies, sausage and hot pepper.

Like other members of the cabbage family, this super food is packed with lots of iron, vitamin C, potassium, calcium and dietary fiber. It also contains lutein, which is an antioxidant that protects the retinas from damage caused by free radicals. Broccoli rabe is chock full of carotenoids and cancer-fighting indoles and isothiocyanates.

Serves 4

Ingredients:

1 pound broccoli rabe, trimmed and chopped into 2-inch pieces
2 tablespoons extra virgin olive oil
Salt and freshly ground pepper to taste

½ cup sun-dried tomatoes packed in oil, rinsed and roughly chopped
2 tablespoons balsamic vinegar

Method:

1. Bring a large pot of water to boil and put in the broccoli rabe. Blanch for a minute until bright green and barely tender. Using a slotted spoon, remove the rabe from the hot water, and place in a large bowl of ice water to stop the cooking. Drain in a colander and gently pat dry.
2. Heat oil in a large skillet over medium-high heat and add the broccoli rabe. Cook for 3 to 4 minutes until tender. Remove from heat.
3. Now stir in sun-dried tomatoes and the balsamic vinegar and season with salt and pepper. Enjoy it tossed with whole wheat pasta.

Grilled Bell Pepper Salad

Watch out for pepper power with this delicious and nutritious grilled pepper salad. Peppers add color to Mediterranean cooking, whether they are used fresh, roasted or dried and ground in sauces and pastes. Light and delicious, peppers pack nutritional goodness.

Peppers are low in calories and contain plenty of nutritious components like vitamins A and C, vitamin K, fiber, folate and beta carotene. Red peppers also contain lycopene, lutein and zeaxanthin which provide protection against macular degeneration.

Serves 4

Ingredients:

4 bell peppers in all colors, halved, seeded and stemmed

¼ cup oil-cured black olives, halved and pitted

¼ cup sun-dried tomatoes packed in oil, rinsed and roughly chopped

1 tablespoon extra virgin olive oil

1 tablespoon balsamic vinegar

Salt to taste

Method:

1. Grill bell peppers on medium-high heat. Make sure to turn them over a few times. Grill until soft and charred in spots, about 3-4 minutes per side. Remove from heat.
2. When they have cooled, chop the peppers. In a large bowl, toss well with olives, oil, sun-dried tomatoes, vinegar and salt.

Steamed Salmon with Avocado

Eating healthy doesn't mean you need to scrimp on flavor, and this Mediterranean style Salmon is indeed loaded with flavors from the deep seas.

With busy lifestyles comes the need to find healthy, flavorful dishes that can be prepared in a short amount time. This salmon dish has high-quality protein, vitamins and minerals including potassium, selenium and vitamin B12. The high content of omega-3 fatty acids contributes to healthy brain function and both heart and joint health.

Serves 4

Ingredients:

4 salmon fillets (1 inch thick; about 3 ounces each)

2 lemons, 1 cut into wedges, 1 cut into thin rounds

1 avocado, halved, pitted, peeled, and thinly sliced

½ cup olive oil

¼ cup balsamic vinegar

4 cloves garlic, crushed

Salt to taste

Method:

1. In a small bowl, mix olive oil with balsamic vinegar.

2. Spread crushed garlic onto the fillets and season with salt. Coat the fillets on both sides with vinegar and oil.
3. Arrange lemon rounds on bottom of your steamer basket and place salmon on top of lemons. Cover with steamer lid.
4. Bring about 1 inch water to boil in a large skillet. Reduce heat and allow it to simmer. Place steamer basket in water, and steam until fish is cooked through, about 5-6 minutes.
5. Arrange avocado and salmon on plates. Serve with lemon wedges.

Pomegranate Farro Tabbouleh Salad

The ruby red pomegranate seeds, bright green parsley leaves and golden raisins add a splash of color to this tasty vegetarian salad. You will feel good while eating it and for a long time after.

Pomegranate seeds and leafy green vegetables have plenty of protein. This dish is packed with healthy carbs, thanks to the whole-grain, fiber-rich farro. Parsley, a pretty little Mediterranean herb, is rich in many vitamins, including vitamins K, B 12, C and A. It helps to keep your immune system strong, strengthens bones and heals the nervous system. Regular consumption of parsley in your diet keeps your blood pressure under control and supports your kidney function by flushing out excess fluids from your body.

Serves 4

Ingredients:

1 cup farro
4 scallions, thinly sliced
½ cup chopped parsley leaves
1 clove garlic, finely chopped
2 large tomatoes, deseeded and chopped into ¼ inch pieces
½ cup chopped mint leaves
1/3 cup golden raisins

1 cup pomegranate seeds
1 small cucumber, peeled and cut into ¼ inch pieces
2 tablespoons fresh lemon juice
2 tablespoons extra virgin olive oil
Salt and freshly ground black pepper to taste

Method:

1. Cook farro as directed on package, and put aside.
2. Place tomatoes, cucumber, scallion, parsley, garlic, mint, raisins, pomegranate seeds, lemon juice, olive oil, salt and pepper into a large bowl. Stir to combine.
3. Add cooked farro to this mixture, and stir well. Set aside at room temperature for 20 minutes before serving.

Halibut Stew

We know that eating plenty of fish and seafood are an important element of the Mediterranean Diet—it helps you lose weight and maintain good health. This gloriously summery fish stew tastes like its right out of a Greek fisherman's boat, and makes for a quick, delicious and satisfying lunch.

Halibut is an excellent source of high quality protein and has significant amounts of other nutrients like vitamin B12, vitamin B6, selenium, potassium, phosphorous, magnesium, niacin, and probably the most important of all – omega-3 fatty acids.

Serves 4

Ingredients:

2 tablespoons extra virgin olive oil

2 onions, peeled and roughly chopped

1 celery rib, trimmed and roughly chopped

5 cloves garlic, peeled and roughly chopped

3 tomatoes, roughly chopped

2 potatoes, peeled and cut into 1 inch cubes

3 bay leaves

4 cups organic vegetable stock

1 ½ pounds firm skinless fillets of Halibut, cut in 2-inch pieces

Juice of 1 lemon

1 small bunch fresh flat-leaf parsley, roughly chopped

1 small bunch fresh dill, roughly chopped

Salt and freshly ground black pepper to taste

Method:

1. Heat olive oil in a large pan over medium heat. Add onion and celery and stir until soft. Then add garlic, and stir until soft, but not brown.
2. Add the tomatoes, potatoes and bay leaves. Stir until the tomatoes are soft. Pour in the stock. Season with salt and pepper and bring it all to a boil. Reduce to a low heat, cover partially and simmer for 15 minutes.
3. Add the fish and bring back to a boil. Reduce to a medium-low heat and simmer for another 10 minutes until the potatoes are tender, and the fish is cooked.
4. Stir in the lemon juice parsley and dill. Drizzle with extra virgin olive oil. Serve with bread.

Linguine with Garlicky Shrimp and Green Beans

The Mediterranean diet, as we know, is based largely on plant-based foods with the occasional land or sea animal thrown in for good measure. A few simple ingredients yield great flavor with amazingly brief prep time. Plenty of garlic, a little wine, Parmesan cheese and fresh basil combine in a briny sauce that together with the shrimp and green beans makes a perfect light lunch.

Green beans are very low in calories and contain no saturated fat. They are a very good source of vitamins, minerals and plant derived micronutrients. They have high levels of vitamin A, vitamin B6 (pyridoxine), thiamin (vitamin B-1), and vitamin C.

Serves 4

Ingredients:

1 (12 ounce) package linguine
2 tablespoons olive oil
1½ teaspoons garlic, minced
1 pound large shrimp, peeled and deveined
1 cup organic vegetable broth

¼ cup dry white wine
¼ teaspoon red pepper, crushed
1 cup green beans, chopped to 1-inch pieces
½ cup Parmesan cheese, shredded
2 tablespoons chopped fresh basil

Method:

1. Cook linguine according to package directions. Drain and keep warm.
2. In a large skillet, heat oil over medium-high heat. Add garlic and sauté. Add broth, wine, and pepper to pan and bring to a boil.
3. Reduce heat, and simmer 5 minutes, stirring occasionally. Add shrimp and green beans to pan; cook for 2 minutes or until thoroughly heated.
4. Add linguine to pan and toss gently. Sprinkle with parmesan and basil when serving.

Greek Salad Pita Pockets with Hummus

The combination of the low-calorie and nutrient-dense leafy greens, tomatoes, onions and cucumbers with the carbs in the pita bread makes this a flavorful and healthy lunch option.

Wonderful crunchy cucumbers, which are a part of this salad, are rich in two of the most basic elements needed for healthy digestion: water and fiber. It is also a healthy source of potassium, Vitamin B and Vitamin K. Consumption of cucumbers protects your brain and fights cancer and inflammation.

Serves 4

Ingredients:

3 tablespoons extra virgin olive oil

1 tablespoon red wine vinegar

2 cloves garlic, smashed

1 tsp dried oregano

1 cup diced seeded peeled cucumber

1 cup chopped green bell pepper

1 ¼ cups plum or cherry tomatoes, seeded and chopped

2/3 cup red onion, chopped

½ cup radishes, chopped

½ cup fresh Italian parsley, chopped

1 cup feta cheese, crumbled

4 8-inch whole wheat pita breads, halved

6 ounces hummus

Salt & pepper to taste

Method:

1. Whisk olive oil, red wine vinegar, dried oregano and garlic in large bowl and season with salt and pepper.
2. In a large bowl, mix tomatoes, cucumber, green bell pepper, red onion, radishes, and parsley. Drizzle the dressing and toss well. Stir in feta cheese.
3. Spread hummus inside the pita pockets generously. Using slotted spoon, transfer salad mixture to pita bread halves. Serve pita pockets immediately.

Roasted Vegetables with Balsamic Vinegar

Brighten up your lunch with this colorful dish. Antioxidant rich veggies, like squash, zucchini and bell peppers, get a flavorful punch from balsamic vinaigrette.

The recipe makes use of the extremely versatile yellow squash, which contains negligible fat and hardly any cholesterol, yet has loads of magnesium, shown to reduce the risk of heart attack and stroke. Yellow squash also has high concentrations of beta carotene and lutein, which is known to prevent macular degeneration and cataracts.

Serves 4

Ingredients:

2 tablespoons balsamic vinegar

½ cup extra virgin olive oil

3 garlic cloves, minced

1 ½ teaspoons fresh thyme, finely chopped

1 teaspoon finely chopped fresh basil

2 large red onions, halved, thinly sliced

1 yellow bell pepper, cut into ½-inch pieces

1 red bell pepper, cut into ½-inch pieces

1 orange bell pepper, cut into ½-inch pieces

1 eggplant, cut into ½-inch slices

1 yellow squash, cut into 1/3-inch-thick rounds

1 zucchini, cut into 1/3-inch-thick rounds

Salt to taste

Method:

1. Preheat oven to 450°F.
2. In a medium sized bowl, whisk vinegar and mustard. Gradually whisk in oil and stir in garlic, thyme, and basil. Season with salt and pepper to taste.
3. Toss onions, yellow, red and orange bell peppers, eggplant, squash and zucchini in large bowl and sprinkle salt and pepper on the mixture. Add dressing; toss to coat. Place on rimmed baking sheets and roast until vegetables are tender and slightly brown around edges.

Anchovy with Broccoli Rabe

Quick to make, yet full of flavors, this easy lunch blends the best of the Mediterranean Diet flavors—garden fresh flavors of broccoli and garlic with the sea-kissed taste of anchovies—to produce a delicious meal worth savoring.

Anchovies are rich in omega-3 fatty acids, iron and magnesium. They are good for the heart, make the bones strong and boost blood cell regeneration. Combine this with the nutritional benefits of the vitamin rich broccoli rabe, and you have a meal that is light in calories yet heavy in health benefits.

Serves 6

Ingredients:

2 pounds broccoli rabe, stem ends trimmed and chopped

6 anchovy fillets, chopped

6 cloves garlic, chopped

3 tablespoons extra virgin olive oil

¼ teaspoon red pepper, crushed

Salt and freshly ground black pepper to taste

Method:

1. Boil water in a large pot. Add broccoli rabe, and cook for 3 to 5 minutes or until tender. Drain the water and set aside.
2. Heat olive oil in a large skillet over medium heat. Add garlic, anchovies and crushed red pepper. Cook for 1 to 2 minutes till garlic is light brown.
3. Add the broccoli rabe and toss to distribute evenly. Season with salt and pepper to taste. This dish is a delight on all its own, but can also be served with pasta or risotto.

CHAPTER 6

Recipes for Dinner

The longevity of the people in the Mediterranean region is well known. The secret to this lies to a large extent in their diet as well as how they eat. Dinner for most Greek and Italians is a time to eat as well as talk. They discuss the day's activities as well as their plans for the next day and also hold philosophical debate. After all, this is the region which produced some of philosophy's greatest minds like Aristotle, Plato and Epicurus, to name just a few.

If you are someone who prefers to eat dinner while simultaneously watching TV, then it might be a good idea to do only one of these activities at a time. When you are eating, it is important to savor the food and to listen to the signals that your body is sending you when you are full. When you are engrossed in something else while eating, you tend to overeat, which is not going to be helpful if you are trying to lose weight. It is not just about eating light but eating right.

Lemon Garlic Shrimp with Asparagus and Bell Peppers

This protein-rich dish features low-calorie shrimp with healthy Mediterranean ingredients including olive oil, garlic, lemon juice and bell peppers. Seafood is a staple protein in the diet of the people in the Mediterranean region. They live lives surrounded by the sea. Any and all kinds of shellfish and fish are enjoyed, often several types in the same dish.

Shrimp are an excellent, carbohydrate-free food for anyone determined to shed pounds because they are loaded with protein, vitamin D, vitamin B3 and zinc. They also have astaxanthin, an antioxidant and anti-inflammatory carotenoid that gives them their pink color and protects your skin from premature aging. The omega-3 fatty acids in shrimp provide antioxidant protection. In addition, shrimp has a copper-containing protein called hemocyanin which can help prevent hair loss, contribute to hair thickness and intensify hair color.

Serves 4

Ingredients:

1 ½ pounds medium shrimp, peeled and deveined

4 teaspoons extra virgin olive oil, divided

5 cloves garlic, minced

2 red bell peppers, diced

2 pounds asparagus, trimmed and cut into 1-inch slices

2 teaspoons freshly grated lemon zest

1 cup reduced-sodium chicken broth

1 teaspoon cornstarch

2 tablespoons lemon juice

2 tablespoons chopped fresh parsley

Salt to taste

Method:

1. Heat 2 teaspoons olive oil in a large skillet over medium-high heat, and add bell peppers, asparagus, lemon zest and salt to taste. Stir occasionally, and transfer the vegetables to a bowl when they have started getting soft.

2. Now heat the remaining 2 teaspoons of oil in the skillet, and add garlic. When it is fragrant, add shrimp, and stir for 1 minute. In a small bowl, whisk broth and cornstarch with some salt to a smooth consistency, and add to the pan.

3. Stir continuously until the sauce has thickened slightly and the shrimp are pink and just cooked through. Remove from heat.

4. Add lemon juice and chopped parsley. Serve the shrimp and sauce over the vegetables.

Goat Cheese Roasted Vegetables

Fruit and nut trees are almost as common as olive trees in the Mediterranean region. Different kinds of nuts such as walnuts, pecans and hazelnuts are savored as snacks, ground into sauces or even sprinkled on salads. The presence of such fresh and healthy ingredients makes this dinner meal a light and flavorful delight.

This nutty dish is loaded with heart-friendly monounsaturated fats derived from the nuts. Nuts are a rich source of flavonoids which support brain health, improve circulation and reduce symptoms associated with allergies. They are also protein rich and high in fiber, vitamin E, folate, calcium and magnesium.

Serves 4

Ingredients:

2 red or orange bell peppers, halved and seeded

5 carrots, trimmed, scrubbed, and halved

4 tablespoons olive oil

1 navel orange, peel and pith removed, sliced

1 clementine, peel and pith removed, sliced

¼ cup fresh goat cheese

¼ cup toasted walnuts, pecans and hazelnuts, chopped

1 tablespoon balsamic vinegar

Salt and freshly ground black pepper to taste

Method:

1. Preheat oven to 425°F.
2. Place peppers and carrots on a baking sheet, drip some olive oil and season with salt and pepper. Roast for about 15 minutes, turning once, until golden brown and tender.
3. Arrange the roasted carrots and peppers with the orange and Clementine on a platter. Sprinkle crumbled goat cheese and hazelnuts.
4. In a small bowl, whisk vinegar and remaining oil, season with salt and pepper and drizzle over vegetables.

Mixed Seafood Risotto

The unique flavor and the health benefits of the Mediterranean Diet comes from the freshness of the ingredients used, especially the seafood. This dinner recipe contains mussels, clams and squid but if you are missing one ingredient, just increase the quantity of another.

Mussels, clams, prawns and squid not only bring an abundance of flavors, they also offer remarkable health benefits. Studies show that people who eat at least one serving of seafood a week reduce their risk of heart disease. Mussels contain the highest level of omega-3 fatty acids among shell fish. All seafood is rich in vitamin B12, which helps you to stay energized.

Serves 6

Ingredients:

2 pounds mussels, scrubbed and cleaned

2 pounds clams, cleaned and soaked in water overnight

1 pound squid, cleaned and cut into rings

1 pound prawns, peeled and deveined

2 cloves garlic, minced

1 cup white wine

1 pound medium-grain carnaroli rice

1 onion, halved and thinly sliced

1 carrot, chopped

1 red pepper, crushed

½ tablespoon black pepper, freshly ground

2 tablespoon olive oil

¼ cup parsley

Salt to taste

Method:

1. Cook the clams and the mussels in two large saucepans with water. Cover and cook for 2 minutes or until they open. Drain the water into a bowl and set aside for cooking the rice. When the clams and mussels have cooled down, remove the shells and discard.
2. Heat olive oil in a saucepan and add chopped carrot and garlic, squid, prawns and red pepper. Add half of the white wine and cook for two minutes or until squid is tender.
3. In a large saucepan, pour olive oil and sauté onions. Add rice, toast it and then add the rest of the white wine. Once wine is absorbed, pour the strained water from the shellfish, and cook until rice is done.
4. Add cooked clams, mussels, squid and prawns to the risotto, and gently toss to distribute evenly. Add salt and black pepper to taste. Sprinkle parsley and serve.

Eggplant and Tomato Pasta Bake

The eggplant is a favored vegetable in Mediterranean cuisine. Versatile in taste and visually appealing, eggplants combined with tomatoes and bell peppers, two other favorite Mediterranean Diet ingredients, make this baked pasta a delightful veggie dinner.

Eggplants are rich in calcium and other minerals. In addition, they contain phytonutrients which improve blood circulation and nourish the brain. Best of all, these vegetable contain very few calories yet they leave you feeling satiated because of their high fiber content. This fiber content is also known to provide protection from cancer.

Serves 6

Ingredients:

1 pound eggplant, cubed
1 pound tomatoes, halved
1 red bell pepper, chopped
1 onion, chopped
8 ounces quinoa rotelle pasta

¼ cup basil, chopped
¼ cup parmesan cheese, grated
2 tablespoon olive oil
½ tablespoon pepper, freshly ground
Salt to taste

Method:

1. Spray a large baking sheet with olive oil and spread out the tomatoes along with the eggplant, bell pepper and onion. Sprinkle salt and pepper. Broil vegetables for 10 minutes or until tender.

2. Prepare pasta al dente as per package directions. Drain water and add pasta and broiled vegetables in a shallow baking dish. Sprinkle parmesan cheese.
3. Heat oven to 375° F, cover and bake the pasta and vegetables for 15 minutes. Sprinkle with basil and serve.

Seared Salmon with Lemon Basil Risotto

For centuries, fishing was the main occupation of the inhabitants of the Mediterranean region. It is no surprise then that most of their meals include some kind of fish or seafood. Salmon occupies pride of place as a delicacy and as a healthy, flavorful choice. This simple combination of salmon with rice is perfect for a light dinner, ideal for those who want to lose weight without compromising on taste.

From nourishing the brain to regulating blood pressure, preventing macular degeneration and diabetes and providing protection from cancer, salmon is a high-protein low calorie ingredient. This fish also provides essential omega-3 fatty acids and plenty of vitamins and minerals. This dinner meal will make you full without worry of weight gain.

Serves 2

Ingredients:

2 salmon fillets, 2 ounces each
½ cup Arborio rice
3 cups water
1 onion, diced
2 green onions, chopped
1 lemon

1 ounce feta cheese
1 cup chicken broth
¼ cup basil, chopped
2 tablespoons olive oil
½ tablespoon pepper, freshly ground
Salt to taste

Method:

1. Pour 1 tablespoon olive oil in a large skillet, and sauté the onions over medium heat for 5 minutes or until tender. Add Arborio rice and toast for 2 minutes. Add water, chicken broth, salt and pepper and cook for 20 minutes or until rice is tender.
2. Cut lemon and squeeze lemon juice over the rice. Add feta cheese and stir gently to distribute the melted cheese evenly.
3. Pour the remaining olive oil in another skillet, and sear the salmon on high heat for 2 minutes on each side. Add the green onions and toss gently.
4. Sprinkle basil and serve seared salmon on top of the risotto.

Slow Cooker Beef Ragout

Meat makes a rare appearance in the Mediterranean Diet. The inhabitants of Greece, Italy, Southern France and other countries along the coast have practiced the policy of moderation, including meat in their meals by consuming it only once or twice a month. Notwithstanding the tempting taste of this beef ragout stew, it makes sense to indulge in it only occasionally.

Beef contains the highest amount of iron of any meat, and the form of this iron content is such that it is easily absorbed by the human body. Beef is also a good source of zinc and the essential vitamin B12. Contrary to popular belief, eating meat in moderation will provide you with energy and is less likely to make you fat when compared to wheat or other food made from grains.

Serves 6

Ingredients:

1 ½ pounds beef stew meat, cut into 1-inch cubes

2 onions cut into wedges

3 carrots, halved and sliced

1 tomato, diced

1 zucchini, halved and sliced

6 ounces fresh green beans, cut into 1-inch pieces

4 cloves garlic, minced

¼ cup thyme, chopped

¼ cup parsley

1 lemon

1 tablespoon olive oil

½ cup beef broth

½ tablespoon black pepper, freshly ground

Salt to taste

Method:

1. Pour 1 tablespoon olive oil into a large skillet and brown meat over medium heat. Transfer meat to a large slow cooker. Add onions, carrots, tomatoes, garlic, thyme, salt and pepper. Pour in the broth and slow cook over medium heat for 3-4 hours.

2. Add zucchini and green beans. Cover and cook for 15 minutes. Cut lemon and squeeze lemon juice over the veggies. Sprinkle parsley and serve with couscous if desired.

Grilled Eggplant Salad with Feta and Walnuts

This light vegetarian dinner combines a favorite Mediterranean Diet ingredient, eggplant, with lettuce and walnuts to produce a refreshing mix of flavors.

Adding walnuts to meals has been found to help people lose weight, especially the "tire" so many have around the waist. Add to this the probiotic digestive benefits of yogurt, the low-calorie but high nutritional value of eggplant, and you have a delicious dinner with no worries about weight gain.

Serves 4

Ingredients:

1 large eggplant, cut into ½-inch round slices

2 hearts of romaine lettuce

1 lemon

1 clove garlic, mashed to a paste

¼ teaspoon cumin, freshly ground

½ cup parsley, chopped

¾ cup feta cheese, crumbled

1/3 cup walnuts

5 tablespoons extra virgin olive oil

¾ cup plain yogurt

½ tablespoon black pepper, freshly ground

Salt to taste

Method:

1. Brush eggplant slices with 3 tablespoons of olive oil, and sprinkle salt and pepper. Grill at medium heat on both sides for 3 minutes. Transfer to a plate, and set aside.

2. Pour the remaining olive oil into a bowl and add yogurt, garlic and cumin. Stir until evenly distributed. Cut lemon and squeeze juice into this mixture, and add parsley. Add salt to taste. Sprinkle walnuts on top.

3. Serve grilled eggplant slices and romaine lettuce with yogurt dressing on top or on the side.

Eggplant Parmigiana

This scrumptious and nourishing dish is believed to have originated in Sicily but is now famous the world over. A traditionally light dish that brings out the versatile flavor of eggplants, parmigiana is amazing when served with a fried egg.

The fiber, vitamins, potassium and flavonoids in eggplant make it a nutritious vegetable that significantly lowers the risk of heart disease. Its low calorie content makes it a great ingredient to prepare a hearty, yet light meal. Tomatoes contain lycopene, a natural antioxidant that is known to prevent cancer, while the calcium and vitamin K in tomatoes contribute to healthy bones.

Serves 4

Ingredients:

3 pounds eggplant, cut into 1-inch thick slices

3 cloves garlic, crushed

1 ½ pounds tomato, diced

1 cup red wine

½ teaspoon dried oregano

½ cup parmesan cheese, grated

½ cup bread crumbs

¼ cup basil leaves

4 tablespoon olive oil

Salt to taste

Method:

1. Heat 2 tablespoons olive oil in a saucepan, and sauté the garlic. Add tomatoes and the red wine. Bring to a boil, and mash the tomatoes. Add the oregano and simmer for 30 minutes, stirring occasionally. Add salt to taste.

2. Use the remaining olive oil to evenly brush a baking dish. Spread a layer of tomato sauce topped with a layer of eggplant. Sprinkle a layer of parmesan cheese. Top it with a layer of tomato sauce, followed by eggplant and parmesan cheese. Finish with a layer of tomato sauce on top and sprinkle bread crumbs and parmesan cheese.

3. Preheat oven to 350° F, and bake for 30 minutes. Allow to cool a bit before serving with the basil sprinkled on top.

Anchovy Puttanesca Pasta

If you fancy a quick yet tastefully tangy dinner, then this puttanesca pasta with anchovies is just what you need.

Tomatoes are good for the heart, bones, kidneys and eyes. They are also rich in antioxidants, beta-carotene and vitamins which regulate cholesterol levels and maintain blood sugar levels. A sulfur compound called allicin in garlic is known to have potent medicinal properties which can provide protection from the common cold as well as reducing the risk of Alzheimer's and dementia.

Serves 4

Ingredients:

2 tablespoons olive oil

1 onion, minced

3 cloves garlic, minced

1 pound anchovies

2 tomatoes, pureed

½ teaspoon red hot pepper, crushed

2 teaspoons dried oregano

¾ cup black olives, pitted and chopped

¼ cup parsley, chopped

1 pound spaghetti

Salt to taste

Method:

1. Heat the olive oil in a large sauce pan, and sauté the onions until tender. Add the anchovies and garlic, and cook for 1 minute.

2. Pour the tomato puree into the sauce pan, and cook for 2 minutes, stirring occasionally. Add oregano, red hot pepper and olives. Stir and set aside.
3. Cook spaghetti al dente as per package instructions.
4. Serve spaghetti with dollops of the tangy sauce sprinkled with parsley.

Mediterranean Deviled Eggs

Combine the nutritional goodness and versatile flavors of anchovies and eggs to prepare a quick light dinner - Mediterranean style.

Eggs are considered a complete source of high quality protein as they contain all the essential amino acids. They are also rich in vitamin and minerals. Though they contain some fat and cholesterol, eating eggs have been known to aid in weight loss by building muscle mass, regulating blood pressure and strengthening bones.

Serves 6

Ingredients:

1 dozen eggs
1 tablespoon anchovy paste
1 tablespoon capers, finely chopped
1 lemon
2 tablespoon olive oil

½ tablespoon black pepper, freshly ground
1 tablespoon parsley, chopped
Salt to taste

Method:

1. Boil the eggs in a large pot filled with water for 15 minutes. Set aside to cool and remove eggshells when they have cooled. Slice the eggs lengthwise. Scoop out the yolks, and place in a bowl.
2. Arrange the egg white halves on a plate.
3. Mash together the egg yolks in the bowl and add the capers, anchovy paste, pepper and olive oil. Cut lemon and squeeze juice. Mix the paste and add salt to taste.
4. Scoop the yolk mixture and fill the egg white halves. Serve with a topping of parsley.

Greek Paidakia Lamb Chops with Roast Potatoes

In *My Big Fat Greek Wedding*, when the groom tells the bride's aunt that he is a vegetarian, she replies, "That's okay. I make lamb." Lamb chops are indeed a Greek delicacy reserved for special occasions, and paidakia is a traditional Greek favorite.

A good source of protein, lamb also contains vitamin B12, essential for generating energy for bodily functions including metabolism and blood cell production. Lamb also provides essential minerals such as zinc. Since consuming lamb will contribute to your saturated fat and calorie intake, consume it sensibly as they do in the Mediterranean region, especially if you are trying to lose weight.

Serves 4

Ingredients:

8 lamb rib chops, about 25 ounces
1 cup olive oil
2 cloves garlic, minced and divided
1 tablespoon thyme, chopped
1 tablespoon rosemary, chopped
½ tablespoon dried oregano

2 lemons
1 ½ tablespoons black pepper, freshly ground
4 potatoes, cut into wedges
1/3 cup water
Salt to taste

Method:

1. Prepare the marinade in a shallow glass baking dish. Pour ¾ cup olive oil, add 1 clove of minced garlic, 1 tablespoon of black pepper powder, the juice of 1 lemon, thyme, rosemary and salt to taste.
2. Rub marinade over the lamb meat, cover and leave in the fridge for at least 3 hours. If you have more time, then marinade the lamb overnight.
3. Place potato wedges on a roasting pan. Pour remaining olive oil into a bowl, add 1 clove minced garlic, ½ tablespoon black pepper powder, the juice of half a lemon and salt to taste. Mix well and pour over the potato wedges.
4. Preheat oven to 350°F, and bake potatoes for 40 minutes. Place the lamb chops in the same oven, add water and bake for another 40 minutes, flipping the chops halfway through the cooking time.
5. Squeeze half a lemon, and sprinkle oregano over the paidakia before serving.

Souvlaki Kebabs With Veggies

A Greek and Cypriot dish that contains succulent pieces of meat skewered and grilled, souvlaki is one of the most popular comfort foods in the Mediterranean region. Traditionally, the dish is made with pork, although lamb, beef, chicken and even fish may be used.

Besides being a delicious source of essential carbohydrates, Pork provides proteins, vital for repairing and maintaining body tissue and muscle mass. An active lifestyle in combination with moderate amounts of pork meat, once or twice a month as in the Mediterranean Diet, can have significant health benefits.

Serves 6

Ingredients:

1 pound boneless pork loin chops, cut into 1-inch cubes

2 lemons

2 tablespoons olive oil

2 cloves garlic, minced

1 teaspoon dried oregano

½ teaspoon black pepper, freshly ground

½ pound cherry tomatoes

2 onions, cut into wedges

1 cucumber, halved lengthwise and sliced into ½-inch thick pieces

Salt to taste

1 cup yogurt

1 pack wooden skewers

Method:

1. Place pork chops into a large bowl. Cut 1 lemon and squeeze the juice over the meat. Add garlic, oregano, salt and pepper. Add 1 tablespoon olive oil. Toss gently to coat the meat with the marinade.
2. Preheat broiler. Line a baking pan with foil and arrange meat pieces evenly. Broil at 145° F for 10 minutes or until meat is slightly pink in the center, turning meat pieces over once. Juice the remaining lemon and pour with olive oil over the pork.
3. Grill the onion wedges, tomatoes and cucumber for 5 minutes. Use a wooden skewer to pierce a piece of pork, a tomato, a cucumber and an onion wedge. Serve with yogurt on the side or tzatziki dip.

Shrimp Saganaki

Pan-fried cheese, cooked in a type of frying pan called a saganaki, is often served as an appetizer in Greece and Turkey. From this tradition of frying cheese in a pan emerged a rich variety of dinner dishes using pan fried seafood like shrimp and mussels. Quick and easy to make, the shrimp saganaki makes for an especially light yet nutritious dinner choice, ideal for those who are serious about controlling or losing weight.

Compared to meat, shrimp contains very few calories. Rich in proteins, vitamin and iron, they help build muscle and aid in weight loss. They also optimize red blood cell production and the distribution of oxygen within the body.

Serves 4

Ingredients:

12 jumbo shrimp, peeled and deveined

1 lemon

1 tablespoon extra virgin olive oil

1 red hot pepper, deseeded and minced

5 green onions, thinly sliced

½ cup white wine

1 cup feta cheese, crumbled

½ tablespoon black pepper, freshly ground

Salt to taste

Method:

1. Cut lemon and squeeze juice over shrimp placed in a bowl. Sprinkle salt to taste, and toss to evenly coat the lemon juice over shrimp.
2. Pour olive oil into a large pan, and sauté the green onions until tender. Add white wine and red hot pepper. Cook for 1 minute.
3. Add the shrimp, cover and cook for 2 minutes or until shrimp is tender.
4. Sprinkle the feta cheese and remove from heat when it begins to melt. Sprinkle freshly ground pepper and serve.

Greek Spanakopita Spinach Pie

A light and crispy pastry that is a popular delicacy in Greek restaurants, the spanakopita or spinach pie makes for a delightful meal.

Spinach contains phytochemicals that have been known to reduce the risk of cancer. Its high water content makes it an extremely filling yet light ingredient. It is a rich source of plant proteins and minerals which have been known to optimize blood circulation and provide stamina for strenuous physical activities.

Serves 4

Ingredients:

2 pounds spinach, chopped

1 onion, chopped

2 green onions, chopped

2 garlic cloves, minced

½ cup parsley, chopped

2 eggs, beaten

½ cup ricotta cheese

1 cup feta cheese, crumbled

8 sheets phyllo dough

½ cup olive oil

Salt to taste

Method:

1. Pour 3 tablespoons olive oil into a large skillet, and sauté the onions, garlic and green onions until tender. Add spinach and parsley, and sauté for 2 minutes. Remove from heat, and set aside.

2. In a bowl, mix the eggs with the ricotta and feta cheese.
3. Preheat oven to 350° F. Brush olive oil lightly onto a baking pan. Lay one sheet of phyllo dough in baking pan and brush lightly with olive oil. Lay 3 more sheets of phyllo dough brushing olive oil on each sheet. Spread the spinach, egg and cheese mixture onto the dough. Fold overhanging edges of the dough sheets over the filling and layer the remaining dough sheets, brushing each sheet with olive oil. Seal the filling on the edges by tucking in the dough sheets.
4. Bake for 40 minutes. Cut and serve warm.

Yemista (Veggie Stuffed Tomatoes)

The name of the dish yemista or gemista in Greek means "stuffed with" and is traditionally a popular dish during Mediterranean summers. Due to the ready availability of tomatoes all year round and the versatile nature of the stuffing, it's a dish you can have anytime. Since it contains the goodness of many vegetables, it makes a satisfying yet low calorie meal.

The lycopene, beta carotene, vitamins and antioxidants in tomatoes make it a very nutritious addition to any meal. Eating tomatoes regularly in your diet contributes to a healthy heart, kidneys and strong bones. Combine this with the low calorie, high vitamin content of bell peppers, and you have superlight yet highly nourishing meal that you can have as often as you want without worrying about weight gain.

Serves 4

Ingredients:

4 large tomatoes
3 green bell peppers
2 eggplants
2 medium zucchinis
2 cloves garlic, minced
1 onion, finely chopped
2 potatoes, cut into wedges

½ cup parsley, chopped
¾ cup olive oil
1 cup water
½ tablespoon black pepper, freshly ground
Salt to taste

Method:

1. Slice off the top of the tomatoes but retain them to use later. Carefully scoop out the pulp and save the pulp in a bowl.
2. Slice off the top of the bell peppers and retain the top. Carefully scoop out the seeds.
3. Cut the eggplants lengthwise and scoop out the pulp using a spoon and add to the tomato pulp. Do the same with the zucchini.

4. Mash and mix the pulp by hand or puree it in a food processor. Add onion, garlic, half the olive oil, salt and pepper.
5. Stuff the pulp mixture, using a spoon, into the tomatoes and bell peppers and use the cut tops as lids.
6. In a baking pan, place the stuffed tomatoes, bell pepper and potato wedges. Pour the rest of the olive oil in, and add 1 cup of water.
7. Bake in a preheated oven at 375°F for 1 hour. Sprinkle parsley on top and serve.

Aginares a la Polita (Constantinople Style Artichokes)

This veritable vegetable stew containing artichokes is believed to have originated in the ancient city of Constantinople. It is one of the Mediterranean Diet recipes that is surprisingly simple to make yet delicious every time you taste it.

Since ancient times, the artichoke has been revered as an aphrodisiac, diuretic, breath freshener and even as a deodorant. Scientific studies confirm the medicinal properties of the vegetable in treating chronic digestive problems and regulating cholesterol levels. An excellent source of dietary fiber and vitamins C and K, they also contain antioxidants, making them effective in boosting the immune system. They have been known to help defend the body against ailments like cancer and heart disease.

Serves 4

Ingredients:

10 artichoke hearts, cut in halves
5 green onions, chopped
10 pearl onions, peeled, stems trimmed and left whole
1 pound potatoes, diced
5 carrots
½ cup olive oil

1 lemon
1 cup chicken broth
½ cup water
½ cup parsley, chopped
½ tablespoon black pepper, freshly ground
Salt to taste

Method:

1. In a large saucepan, pour half the olive oil and sauté the green onions until tender. Add the pearl onions, carrots and potatoes, and sauté for 5 minutes.
2. Add in the juice of one lemon, the chicken broth, water and the remaining olive oil to the saucepan and bring to a boil. Simmer and cook for 20 minutes, stirring occasionally or until vegetables are tender.

3. Add artichokes and season with pepper and salt. Cover and cook for 15 minutes on simmer or until artichokes are tender.
4. Garnish with parsley and serve.

Mila Gemista Me Kima (Beef Stuffed Apples)

Trust the Greeks to experiment and combine diverse ingredients in an exciting way. This is a unique Mediterranean Diet dish in the sense that it combines the sweetness of a fruit with the irresistible flavors of ground beef, nuts and spices to create a culinary masterpiece.

There's hardly anyone in the medical or health community who would deny the health benefits of eating apples. Besides being a well-known source of dietary fiber and vitamins, there's evidence to suggest that apples have a role in helping people lose weight when consumed on a regular basis. This mila gemista me kima recipe just gave you another delicious reason to have apples.

Serves 4

Ingredients:

4 apples
½ pound beef, ground
¼ cup olive oil
1 onion, finely chopped
2 tablespoons parsley, chopped
¼ cup of pine nuts

¼ cup raisins
1 cup beef stock
½ tablespoon cinnamon, freshly ground
2 tablespoons butter
Salt to taste

Method:

1. Slice the top of each apple and discard. Carefully scoop out the core and flesh from inside the apple, to create a deep and wide hollow. Blanch the hollow apples in boiling water for 3 minutes.
2. In a pan, heat olive oil, and sauté onions till tender. Add meat and cook over medium heat until light brown. Add cinnamon, parsley, beef stock, salt and pepper and simmer for 15 minutes. Add pine nuts and raisins.
3. Preheat oven to 400°F. Fill apples with the meat mixture and place in a baking dish. Bake for 30 to 45 minutes. Let cool for 10 minutes before serving.

Kotopoulo me bamies (Chicken Stew with Okra)

Okra, called bamies in Greek, is considered one of the best complements to any meat dish. This simple yet inventive dish combines the perennial favorite of many home cooks, chicken, with the distinct taste of okra to produce a uniquely nourishing dinner.

Favored among nutrition experts as a nourishing ingredient in weight control or weight loss diets, okra is a rich source of dietary fiber, minerals and vitamins with no saturated fat or cholesterol. Rich in iron, calcium, manganese and magnesium, the vegetable also contains vitamin K which helps strengthen bones. Okra is rich in vitamin C, which is known to help boost the immune system and provide protection from all kinds of common infections as well as serious diseases like cancer and heart disease.

Serves 4

Ingredients:

4 pounds chicken
1 pound okra, stems removed
1 pound tomatoes, chopped
1 onion, chopped
1 cup olive oil

1 cup white wine vinegar
1 cup water
½ tablespoon black pepper, freshly ground
Salt to taste

Method:

1. Place the okra in a bowl, and add vinegar. Gently toss to coat the vinegar over the okra evenly. Transfer to a strainer and set aside for about an hour.
2. Pour ¼ cup olive oil into a large skillet, and fry the okra for 3 minutes. Remove okra and set aside. In the same skillet, pour ¼ cup olive oil and fry the chicken until golden brown.
3. In a sauce pan, pour ½ cup olive oil, and sauté the onions until tender. Add tomatoes and 1 cup of water and bring to a boil. Add chicken, cover and cook on simmer for 50 minutes or until chicken is tender. Add salt and pepper. Add the okra and stir gently to mix just before serving.

Orange, Anchovy and Olive Salad

This Italian delicacy brings together an unlikely but immensely satisfying combination of fruits, seafood and herbs. It's another example of healthy indulgence that you will find only in the Mediterranean Diet.

The vitamin C content in oranges help boost the immune system while a nutrient known as choline is known to aid in sleep regulation, muscle movement and improving cognitive skills. Oranges also contain polyunsaturated fat and omega-3 fatty acids which promote a healthy heart, as well as better skin, stronger muscle tissue and better eyesight. In addition, onions are a potent weapon to combat disease as well as an effective diet tool to lose weight.

Serves 4

Ingredients:

4 oranges, peeled and sliced into thin rounds

6 anchovy fillets

1 onion, sliced into thin rings

½ cup black olives, pitted and halved

1 lemon

3 tablespoons extra virgin olive oil

½ tablespoon black pepper, freshly ground

Salt to taste

Method:

1. Arrange the round orange slices on a large platter. Place the onion rings over the orange slices, and sprinkle the olives over them.
2. Layer the top with anchovy fillets. Cut and squeeze a lemon, and drizzle the olive oil on top.
3. Sprinkle salt and pepper. Before serving, let the salad stand for 30 minutes at room temperature so that the flavors can mingle and develop.

Sardine Salad

After a long day, the last thing you want to do is prepare an elaborate dinner. This doesn't mean that you have to eat a pizza that will pack on the pounds. Though the Mediterranean Diet recommends fresh ingredients, sardines even in a can, have significant nutritional value.

Just as the apple is the undisputed nutritional king among fruits, sardines are arguably the preeminent fruit of the sea. Rich in omega-3 fatty acids, sardines provides generous amounts of the essential yet rare vitamin D which enhances the body's ability to absorb calcium from food. From building healthy bones to improving skin health and vision, sardines also offer protection from cholesterol and heart disease.

Serves 4

Ingredients:

½ pound sardines in tomato sauce, canned

½ cup black olives, pitted and halved

1 lettuce, chopped

1 tablespoon olive oil

1 tablespoon red wine vinegar

Method:

1. Spread the lettuce in a bowl. Sprinkle olives and add the sardines. Pour olive oil and red wine vinegar into the bowl.
2. Toss gently to spread the ingredients evenly, and presto, your salad is ready.

Tuscan Chicken

Style and substance come together in this simple yet delicious Italian preparation. This Mediterranean Diet recipe presents a refreshingly unique and healthy way to enjoy chicken.

Protein-rich chicken helps build bone strength and muscle mass. The presence of tryptophan and vitamin B5 in chicken is also known to help provide relief from stress.

Serves 4

Ingredients:

4 boneless chicken breast halves
1 green bell pepper, julienned
1 red bell pepper, julienned
1 yellow bell pepper, julienned
2 cloves garlic, minced
1 tomato, diced

2 tablespoons olive oil
½ tablespoon black pepper, freshly ground
¼ cup chicken broth
¼ cup basil, chopped
Salt to taste

Method:

1. Pour 1 tablespoon olive oil in a large skillet and brown chicken. Sprinkle with pepper. Remove and set aside.
2. In the same skillet, pour the remaining olive oil, and sauté bell peppers until tender. Add garlic and cook for a minute. Add tomatoes, chicken breasts, chicken broth and basil. Bring to a boil. Cover and simmer for 15 minutes or until chicken is tender.

Skillet Prawns in Feta Cheese

Indulging in food to your heart's content yet remaining healthy is one of the main benefits of following a Mediterranean Diet. This simple preparation of prawns with feta cheese proves that it's not really very hard to stay healthy.

Made from goat's milk, feta cheese has a very strong flavor. It has a smaller amount of fat and calories than most other cheeses. Feta also provides essential calcium, vitamins and other minerals. Prawns are rich in omega-3 fatty acids which improve brain function and reduce the risk of cancer, heart disease and arthritis. Prawns also contain unsaturated fat which is known to regulate blood cholesterol levels.

Serves 4

Ingredients:

1 pound prawns, peeled and deveined	¼ cup white wine
1 onion, finely chopped	2 tablespoons parsley, chopped
3 tomatoes, diced	¾ cup feta cheese, crumbled
3 cloves garlic, minced	½ teaspoon black pepper, freshly ground
1 tablespoon olive oil	Salt to taste
1 teaspoon dried oregano	

Method:

1. Pour 1 tablespoon olive oil into a large skillet, and sauté onions over medium heat until tender. Add garlic, oregano, tomatoes, salt and pepper. Cook for 1 minute and add white wine. Bring to a boil and simmer for 5 minutes.
2. Add the prawns, and cook for 2 minutes or until prawns turn pink. Sprinkle feta cheese and parsley.
3. Serve warm.

Mediterranean Pork with Orzo

When you want to have a complete meal but are running short on time, this Mediterranean style pork with orzo is just what you need. Quick to make yet very filling, it's a favored healthy dinner choice for the modern hectic lifestyle.

When trying to lose weight, it is a good idea to eat pork tenderloin in moderation because it is an excellent source of lean protein as well as vitamin B12, which helps in converting food to energy. Pork meat also contains healthy amounts of zinc which is required to synthesize proteins, as well as selenium which supplies antioxidants which regulate hormone production.

Serves 4

Ingredients:

1 pound pork tenderloin, cut into 1-inch cubes	1 cup orzo pasta
5 grape tomatoes, halved	¾ cup feta cheese, crumbled
6 ounces baby spinach	1 teaspoon black pepper, freshly ground
2 tablespoons olive oil	Salt to taste

Method:

1. Sprinkle pepper over the pork. Heat olive oil in a large skillet, and cook pork for 10 minutes or until no longer pink. Add tomatoes, and cook for 1 minute.
2. Cook orzo pasta as per package directions.

3. Add spinach to pasta and cook for a minute before draining.
4. Stir in pasta over pork and sprinkle feta cheese before serving.

Greek Pastitsio Baked Pasta

Traditionally, the Greeks ate meat on rare occasions, once or twice per a month, and their health and life longevity is definitely influenced by this low meat intake.

A good source of protein, iron, zinc and vitamin B12, beef is a healthy ingredient in any dietary plan when consumed in moderation. Cheese is highly nutritious and provides healthy amounts of calcium, protein, zinc, vitamins A and B12. Eating cheese has been known to contribute to building strong bones and muscle mass.

Serves 6

Ingredients:

1 pound ground beef
1 onion, chopped
2 tomatoes, chopped
2 cloves garlic, minced
6 eggs
4 tablespoons olive oil

8 ounces fettuccine
½ teaspoon cinnamon, freshly ground
1/8 teaspoon ground nutmeg
1/3 cup parmesan cheese, grated
¼ cup feta cheese, crumbled
½ cup ricotta cheese, crumbled

Method:

1. Heat 2 tablespoons of olive oil in a skillet, and sauté onion until tender. Add ground beef, garlic, tomatoes, cinnamon and nutmeg. Simmer for 5 minutes.
2. Cook pasta in water for 1 minute. Drain undercooked pasta and put in a pan. Sprinkle parmesan cheese. Break 2 eggs and add to the pan to coat the pasta.
3. In a food processor bowl, mix feta, ricotta and 4 eggs to get a smooth texture.
4. Preheat oven to 400°F. Brush baking dish liberally with olive oil and spread pasta. Pour beef mixture over pasta and spread evenly. Bake for 5 minutes.
5. Add the cheese mixture cheese to the pasta, and bake for 10 minutes or until top is golden brown. Serve warm.

Chicken Saltimbocca

Enjoy this classic Italian chicken dish for a lightweight dinner. You will be tempted to eat it more often consider how convenient and easy it is to prepare. Buon appetito.

Eating chicken helps build muscles and strengthen bones. As a source of lean protein, it is a healthy ingredient to energize and control your weight. The abundant use of lemon juice in the Mediterranean Diet has contributed to the disease-free, life longevity that people in the region enjoy. Lemon juice is well-known for its therapeutic properties, which include strengthening the immune system, purifying the blood and cleansing the stomach.

Serves 4

Ingredients:

4 boneless skinless chicken breast halves	1 tablespoon butter
8 fresh sage leaves	1 ½ tablespoon olive oil
8 thin prosciutto slices	2 tablespoons white wine
1 lemon	½ cup chicken broth
½ cup all-purpose flour	Salt and pepper to taste

Method:

1. Sprinkle salt and pepper on chicken. Over each chicken piece, place 2 sage leaves. Place 2 prosciutto slices over each piece and press down gently.
2. Place the chicken pieces on a plate and sprinkle flour over them. Turn the chicken pieces to coat with flour on both sides.
3. In a large skillet, melt butter over medium heat. Place the chicken pieces with the prosciutto side facing down. Cook for 4 minutes. Turn the chicken pieces and cook for 4 minutes. Transfer to a plate and set aside.
4. Pour chicken broth in the same skillet. Add the lemon juice and white wine, and bring to a boil. Add salt and pepper to taste. Pour the sauce over the chicken pieces and serve with orzo.

Testi Kebab Casserole

In Turkey, meat was traditionally cooked in covered earthen pots which imparted a special flavor to the dish. This spicy version of a traditional Mediterranean Diet stew from Turkey combines traditional ingredients with the convenience of modern cooking.

In the Mediterranean Diet, meat is consumed only on rare occasions and this practice of moderation has contributed to the overall health of the people living in the region. Grass-fed goat meat is an excellent source of lean protein, containing essential amino acids which contribute effectively to building muscle mass, strengthening body tissues and improving bone strength.

Serves 4

Ingredients:

2 pounds goat meat, cut into 1-inch pieces

5 onions, chopped

5 potatoes, diced

3 tomatoes, diced

1 teaspoon red hot pepper, crushed

1 teaspoon black pepper, freshly ground

1 teaspoon cinnamon, freshly ground

1 teaspoon cumin, freshly ground

4 cups water

4 teaspoons olive oil

Salt to taste

Method:

1. Place the goat into a large bowl. Add onion, potatoes and tomatoes. Sprinkle the red hot pepper, black pepper, cinnamon and cumin onto the mutton. Add salt to taste. Mix to combine the spices with the goat and vegetables. Add olive oil.
2. Preheat oven to 400°F. Transfer the goat and veggies to a large casserole dish. Add water, cover and bake in the oven for 2 hours.

Kolokithakia Gemista (Stuffed Zucchini)

Centuries of cultural exchange between Greece and Turkey has produced an interesting mixture of dishes. This meat-stuffed zucchini preparation is equally popular in both countries.

The protein in the veal combined with the low-calorie nature of zucchini makes this an ideal choice for a light dinner. Zucchini is chock full of dietary fiber. The vegetable is especially favored among health experts and nutritionists for preventing constipation and boosting the immune system.

Serves 4

Ingredients:

8 zucchini

2 pounds veal, ground

3 cloves garlic, minced

1 lemon

4 tablespoons olive oil

1 cup long-grain rice

½ teaspoon black pepper, freshly ground

½ cup mint leaves, finely chopped

1 cup Greek yogurt

Salt to taste

Method:

1. Cut the ends of the zucchini and scoop out the flesh using a long spoon.

2. In a bowl, place the ground veal. Add rice, salt and pepper and mix thoroughly. Stuff the zucchinis with the meat and rice mixture.
3. Place the stuffed zucchinis in a casserole and add water so that the level just reaches the mouth or opening of the zucchini. Pour olive oil, cover and cook on medium heat for 40 minutes.
4. In a bowl, add the garlic to the yogurt. Cut and squeeze lemon juice and sprinkle mint leaves over the yogurt. Mix to get an even texture.
5. Serve the stuffed zucchinis warm with a generous amount of yogurt sauce on the side.

Quinoa Tabbouleh

Tabbouleh is a classic Middle Eastern dish popular in Lebanon and Turkey. Traditionally prepared using bulgur, this quinoa version is particularly beneficial for those who are trying to control or lose weight. Gluten-free and completely vegetarian, it's also an easy dinner to prepare.

A good source of protein, calcium, magnesium and manganese as well as vitamins and dietary fiber, quinoa is hailed as one of the healthiest ingredients for a health conscious diet. The density of dietary fiber makes it a low-GI carbohydrate. It also contains omega-3 fatty acids and anti-inflammatory phytonutrients.

Serves 4

Ingredients:

1 cup quinoa, rinsed, soaked and drained
1 pint cherry tomatoes, halved
2 green onions, thinly sliced
2 cucumbers, diced
1 lemon
1 clove garlic, minced
½ cup extra virgin olive oil

½ tablespoon black pepper, freshly ground
2/3 cup parsley, chopped
½ cup mint leaves, finely chopped
1 ¼ cup water
Salt to taste

Method:

1. In a large saucepan, bring water to a boil. Simmer and add quinoa. Cover and cook for 10 minutes. Open cover and fluff cooked quinoa using a fork. Set aside.
2. Pour olive oil in bowl. Add lemon juice, garlic, salt and pepper, and whisk gently.
3. In a large bowl, combine quinoa with tomatoes, onions, cucumbers, parsley and mint. Drizzle olive oil dressing and serve.

Shakshuka Poached Eggs in Tomato Sauce

This egg and tomato combination is a perennial favorite from Israel. Ideal for breakfast, lunch or dinner, it provides a sumptuously filling meal.

Eggs provide proteins, vitamins and minerals such as zinc, copper and iron. Their nutritional value is complemented by the tomatoes, which are rich in antioxidants, beta-carotene and vitamins which regulate cholesterol. The lycopene in tomatoes provide protection from cancer. They also provide multiple nutritional benefits for the heart, bones, muscles, kidneys and eyes.

Serves 4

Ingredients:

8 eggs
2 onions, chopped
1 bell pepper, chopped
2 tomatoes, chopped
4 cloves garlic, chopped
¼ cup tomato puree

1 tablespoon cumin
½ tablespoon black pepper, freshly ground
3 tablespoons olive oil
Salt to taste

Method:

1. Heat olive oil in a large skillet, and sauté onions for 5 minutes or until tender.
2. Add tomato puree, bell pepper, tomatoes and garlic, and cook for 2 minutes. Add cumin powder, pepper and salt to taste.
3. Crack the eggs into the tomato mixture and poach for 10 minutes. Remove from skillet and enjoy.

Tunisian Chickpeas and Vegetable Tagine

The tagine is a very versatile dinner dish that works equally well with both meat and vegetable ingredients. This vegetarian version presents a nutritious combination of legumes, vegetables and spices.

Also known as garbanzo beans, chickpeas are actually legumes. They have a high-fiber content. As a gluten-free plant protein, they are an especially nutritious ingredient in vegetarian meals. They have exceptionally high amounts of iron, vitamin B-6 and magnesium. Their health benefits include prevention of constipation and reducing the risk of diabetes and cancer. They are an ideal tool for weight management because after eating chickpeas, you feel fully satiated and are unlikely to overeat.

Serves 6

Ingredients:

14 ounces chickpeas

2 onions, chopped

2 carrots, sliced

2 tomatoes, chopped

1 pound zucchini, diced

3 cloves garlic, minced

1 lemon

1 tablespoon olive oil

1 teaspoon cinnamon, freshly ground

1 teaspoon cumin, freshly ground

1 cup water

½ teaspoon black pepper, freshly ground

Salt to taste

Method:

1. Heat olive oil in a large saucepan over medium heat, and sauté the onions and carrots for 10 minutes or until tender. Add garlic, cinnamon, cumin, salt and pepper.

2. Add tomatoes and zucchini. Add lemon juice and water, and bring to a boil. Simmer for 20 minutes. Plate and serve.

CHAPTER 7

Recipes for Desserts, Snacks and Beverages

The Mediterranean Diet is based on the joy of eating. There is no guilt associated with eating. Unlike today, when you indulge in an ice cream or a sweet dessert after dinner, the inhabitants of the Mediterranean Region were not unduly worried about the calories. Perhaps this was due to their active lifestyle or the fact that most of the ingredients they used were natural and organic.

Eating desserts after a meal or having a snack in between meals is not something you should feel guilty about. Indeed, it is something you should enjoy. If you adapt a lifestyle that includes a healthy amount of physical activity and reduce your consumption of processed food, then you can also enjoy indulging in healthy desserts and snacks like the Greeks and Italians do.

Desserts

Yiaourti Me Meli (Yogurt, Honey and Walnuts)

In typical Greek tradition, finishing a meal with this yogurt and honey does wonders for the digestion. As a simple dessert, this wonderful combination of Greek yogurt, natural honey and walnuts is a healthy and nutritious after-dinner treat.

The combination of Greek yogurt and honey at the end of a meal get the digestive juices flowing. Yogurt contains probiotics, live microorganisms that help improve digestion and fortify the immune system. Besides aiding in digestion, honey helps the body absorb calcium more effectively, soothes sore throats and also aids in sleep. A compound called tryptophan in honey, triggers the production of serotonin and melatonin, hormones responsible for regulating sleep. Eat well, sleep well, live well.

Serves 4

Ingredients:

2 cups Greek yogurt

¾ cup honey

1 ½ cup walnuts

½ tablespoon cinnamon, freshly ground

Method:

1. Toast the walnuts in a skillet on medium heat for 3 minutes. Set aside.
2. In a bowl, stir in Greek yogurt and add cinnamon powder. Whisk to combine.
3. Add toasted walnuts and pour honey over the mixture.
4. Refrigerate and take out a few minutes before serving.

Ginger Watermelon Sorbetto

Quenching, refreshing and light in calories, this Italian dessert uses fresh natural ingredients to produce an easy to make and delicious dessert.

The presence of the amino acid L-citruline in watermelon is believed to aid in reducing muscle soreness and speed up recovery from strenuous physical activity or exercise. The fruit has high water and fiber content which boosts the digestive process and prevents constipation. Extremely low in calories but rich in nutrients such as vitamins, minerals and antioxidants, it is difficult if not impossible to have too much of a good thing such as the watermelon.

Serves 8

Ingredients:

6 cups of watermelon pulp, seedless and chopped

3 ounces ginger root, peeled and crushed

1 cup honey

1 cup water

¼ cup mint leaves

1 lemon

Method:

1. In a saucepan, heat 1 cup water, and add crushed ginger and honey. Stir, and bring to a boil. Set aside to cool.
2. In a food processor, puree the watermelon pulp. Cut and squeeze lemon juice and add the ginger-honey syrup. Blend and refrigerate. Serve topped with a mint leaf or two.

Banana Pineapple Gelato

If you think gelato is simply ice cream in Italian, think again. This dairy-free, gluten-free, fruity and tangy frozen dessert is among the healthiest and tastiest desserts you will ever have.

Eating pineapples has been associated with a reduced risk of obesity, diabetes and heart disease. Pineapple has a high water content and is also a good source of fiber which aids in digestion and prevents constipation. Bananas contain potassium, which is linked to maintaining healthy heart functions. They also contain healthy amounts of vitamin A as well as beta-carotene and alpha-carotene which helps protect the eyes and improves overall vision.

Serves 8

Ingredients:

4 bananas
½ pineapple, peeled and cored
1 lemon

¾ cup honey
½ tablespoon cinnamon, freshly ground
¼ cup mint leaves

Method:

1. In a food processor, puree bananas and pineapple pulp. Cut and squeeze fresh lemon juice, and add cinnamon and honey. Blend and freeze.
2. Remove from freezer 30 minutes before serving. Scoop and serve with a garnish of mint leaves.

Stewed Apricots with Yogurt and Honey

In the Mediterranean Diet, dessert often consists of a simple bowl of fresh fruits. This dessert choice is as simple as it is refreshing and delicious.

This Mediterranean inspired combo offers a good dose of vitamins A and C, calcium, zinc, and makes a delicious, healthy dessert that can be made ready in a jiffy.

Serves 2

Ingredients:

2 ripe apricots, halved and pitted
¾ cup water
1 teaspoon sugar
1 tablespoon lemon juice
A pinch of cinnamon, crushed

¾ cup Greek yogurt
1 tablespoon honey
1 tablespoon toasted pistachios, roughly chopped

Method:

1. Heat water in a small saucepan and add sugar and lemon juice. Keep stirring to combine, and bring to a boil. Reduce heat, and add the apricots. Cover the pot, and simmer for 30 minutes.
2. Top each stewed apricot with 2 tablespoons of the yogurt. Sprinkle with cinnamon powder and pistachios and drizzle on some honey.

Warm Cinnamon Spiced Fresh Oranges with Honey

Orange slices drenched in honey and cinnamon make a zesty dessert that will leave you feeling like you are on the sunny shores of the Mediterranean.

Choline, a nutrient found in oranges, is involved in regulating sleep cycles and improving muscle movement. The fruit also contains a healthy amount of vitamin C which boosts the immune system and aids in protecting the body from many common infections.

Serves 2

Ingredients:

2 navel oranges
2 tablespoons honey
1 cinnamon, powdered

1 tablespoon orange juice
2 tablespoons sliced pistachios and almonds, lightly toasted

Method:

1. Peel the oranges, and slice the whole fruit into round slices. Arrange these slices in a flat dish.
2. In a saucepan, warm the honey, cinnamon powder, and orange juice over low heat, stirring continuously. Allow the sauce to simmer.
3. Pour the hot sauce over the oranges, and refrigerate.
4. Sprinkle almonds on top before serving.

Dried figs, dates and almond balls

In this delicious Mediterranean dessert, the slight salty taste of almonds mingle with the sweetness of dates and figs. These flavors are made more complex and intriguing by the addition of honey and cinnamon, making this a completely irresistible dessert.

Dried figs are calcium rich as well as high in fiber, manganese, magnesium and potassium. The high dietary fiber content helps reduce hunger cravings and is highly recommended if you are trying to lose weight. The presence of probiotics also helps in improving digestive functions.

Serves 2

Ingredients:

1 cup salted, roasted almonds

1 cup figs, soaked in water for a few hours

1 cup mejdool dates, deseeded

¼ teaspoon cinnamon powder

¼ cup raw sesame seeds

Method:

1. Grind almonds coarsely in a food processor. Squeeze out excess water, and add figs, dates, honey and cinnamon powder. Blend until uniformly mixed.
2. Form the dough into small balls, and roll in a bowl of sesame seeds.

Loukoumades

Loukoumades are little light, bite-sized traditional Greek doughnuts. They are made using a handful of everyday ingredients – flour, yeast, sugar and water.

These golden puffs of delight are served throughout Greece following a long tradition of being served to the winners of the earliest Greek Olympics Games.

Serves 2

Ingredients:

7 ounces self-rising flour

2 ounces corn starch

10 ounces water

1 ½ tablespoons dry active yeast

3 tablespoons honey, divided

5 tablespoons chopped walnuts for garnish

A pinch of cinnamon powder

Salt to taste

2 cups vegetable oil

Method:

1. Dissolve the yeast in the water, and wait until it starts to bubble.
2. Combine the flour, corn starch and salt in a separate bowl and slowly mix it with the yeast and water. Add 2 tablespoons of honey. Whisk until it forms a smooth batter. Cover with plastic wrap, and allow the dough rise for about 1 hour.
3. Heat the oil in a saucepan on the stove until very hot. Test the temperature by adding a drop of the dough to the saucepan. The oil is hot enough if the dough sizzles.

4. Coat a tablespoon with oil, and use it to spoon out some dough. Slowly, drop it into the hot oil. Continue dropping more until the saucepan is full of doughnuts without them touching each other.

5. Move the honey puffs around the hot oil using a slotted spoon, and turn them around so that they are golden brown on all sides. Remove from the hot oil and place them aside on paper towels to drain.

6. Place the loukoumades on a large serving platter. Add honey, cinnamon powder and chopped walnuts.

Maltese Cherry Tart

Revive the flavors of Malta with this thin, cookie-like tart that has a traditional lattice crust and classic combination of cherries and hazelnuts.

Eating hazelnuts can aid in improved metabolism and help you burn calories more effectively. They also have a high protein and fiber composition which helps you feel satiated and reduces hunger cravings.

Serves 4

Ingredients:

For preparing sweet pastry

1 cups all purpose flour ½ cup unsalted butter
¼ cup sugar 1 egg
½ teaspoon salt

For cherry filling

¼ cup cherry preserves Zest of a quarter of a lemon
¼ cup fresh cherries, chopped ¼ cup hazelnuts, chopped

For glaze

1 large egg 1 tablespoon whole milk
1 teaspoon cherry preserve 1 tablespoon sugar

Method:

For sweet pastry

1. Mix flour with sugar and salt in processor and blend for 10 has a fine consistency. Add egg and process on low speed until blended. The dough will be crumbly at this stage. Press it together into two balls; wrap both balls tightly with plastic wrap and chill in the refrigerator for an hour until firm enough to roll.

2. After an hour, take one ball of dough and roll it out on a lightly floured surface and transfer to a loose-bottomed tart tin. The pastry may crack since it is quite fragile. Just patch it with the trimmings, ensuring there are no holes.

For filling
1. Preheat the oven 400°F.
2. Mix fresh cherries, preserves and zest in a bowl.
3. Add the filling into the pastry case and sprinkle with hazelnuts. Roll out second dough ball on lightly floured surface and cut it into strips. Arrange several strips, spaced half an inch apart. Top with more strips at slight angle, so that you form a lattice. Press the ends of the strips to the edge of pan, in a manner that the trims hang.

For glaze
1. Beat egg with the milk and cherry preserve in small bowl to blend. Lightly brush over pastry and sprinkle sugar.
2. Bake tart for about 45 minutes until crust is golden brown. Cool tart completely on a wire rack.

Dried Figs Stuffed with Almonds

This sumptuously chewy, rustic Italian classic can be stored in an air-tight glass jar, separated by some bay leaves that in addition to helping to preserve them, also add a lovely flavor.

Figs contain calcium which helps build bone density and prevents osteoporosis. They also help regulate blood pressure, improve metabolism rates and contribute to reduced hunger cravings, one of the many reasons why they are recommended in weight-loss and weight-control diets.

Serves 2

Ingredients:

10 Dried Figs
20 Almonds, each split into 2

1 teaspoon lemon zest

Method:

1. Preheat the oven to 200°F.
2. Wash the figs in warm water and dry.
3. Cut the figs in half, horizontally, ensuring you still leave the two halves slightly attached. Snip off the top stem.

4. Carefully open each fig. Try not to break it apart and place some lemon zest and 4 almond halves inside.
5. Place them on a flat surface and press them with the heel of your hand.
6. Line them up on a baking sheet and bake for 50 minutes or until they turn golden brown.

Peaches in Cinnamon Spiced Wine

Pesche al vino is a classic Italian summer dessert that is simple to prepare, yet is a refreshing drink that can bring to mind the cool sea spray on a blisteringly hot summer's day.

Peaches contain bioactive and phenolic compounds such as anthocyanins, chlorogenic acids, quercetins and catechins which have been found to possess anti-obesity and anti-inflammatory properties. They also contribute to reduced risk of heart disease and regulate blood cholesterol levels. The presence of resveratrol in red wine is believed to contribute to weight loss by imitating the benefits of exercise, including improved physical stamina and muscle strength.

Serves 2

Ingredients:

2 peaches
1 cup red wine
2 tablespoons lemon juice

1 tablespoon honey
¼ teaspoon cinnamon, ground

Method:

1. Wash the peaches and cut them into 8 slices. Dip them in the lemon juice as soon as you cut them in order to prevent oxidation.
2. Pour the wine in a bowl, and add cinnamon and sugar. Mix until the sugar dissolves.
3. Add the peaches to the wine. Cover and place in the refrigerator for at least 3-4 hours. Serve the peaches in frosted wine glass, and cover them with wine.

Snacks

Warm Cherries topped with Almonds and Cheese

The creamy texture and taste of ricotta, a mild and creamy Italian cheese, is a great partner for sweet red cherries, which are traditionally popular in the Mediterranean region.

In spite of their tiny size, cherries provide a variety of nutrients including vitamins A, C and B and minerals like potassium, calcium, phosphorus, iron and copper.

Serves 2

Ingredients:

1½ cup frozen pitted cherries
4 tablespoons part-skim ricotta
1 tablespoon honey

4 tablespoon almonds, toasted and slivered

Method:

1. Cook cherries and honey over medium-high heat in a skillet. Stir occasionally, about 3-4 minutes.
2. Top the warmed cherries with ricotta and almonds.
3. Serve with a bagel or with graham crackers.

Chickpea Patties with Tahini Sauce

Chickpea patties are known as falafel in the Middle East.. This hearty, healthy snack can be served hot or cold. Served with tahini and pita bread, it makes for one of the most nutritious meals you can have while still delighting in wonderful flavor.

High in calcium and protein, sesame seeds are also an excellent source of copper, zinc, iron, manganese and amino acids. They also contain omega-3 and omega-6 fatty acids which help fight inflammation, provide cardiovascular support and boost the immune system.

Serves 4

Ingredients:

Chickpea patties

2 15 ounce cans of chickpeas, drained
2 teaspoons cumin

2 tablespoons fresh cilantro, chopped
3 garlic cloves, crushed

1 fresh green chili, deseeded and finely chopped

5 tablespoons olive oil

Salt to taste

Tahini Sauce

1 cup of sesame seeds

1/3 cup olive oil

1 clove garlic

½ cup water

½ cup lemon juice

Salt to taste

Sandwich

Shredded lettuce

Tomato wedges

Sliced red onion

Sliced cucumbers

4 pitas, sliced open and lightly toasted

1 cup Greek yogurt

Method:

1. Allow the chickpeas to dry slightly then puree coarsely in a food processor. Add coriander, cumin, garlic and chili to form a thick paste. In case you don't own a food processor, smash the chickpeas using a fork. Season and divide into equal size balls or flattened patties.

2. Heat a little oil in a frying pan, and fry the patties on both sides until crisp and golden.

3. For the tahini sauce, start by preparing the base of the sauce, a paste made from ground sesame seeds and olive oil. Heat a skillet over medium high heat, and add the sesame seeds, stirring frequently as they can burn very easily. Remove from heat when they turn golden brown.

4. When cool, add to a food processor with 3 tablespoons of olive oil and process till it becomes a smooth paste. You can add more olive oil depending on how thick or how thin you want the paste.

5. Now, mash the garlic and add a little salt. Stir this into the tahini. Add lemon juice and some water if you want the sauce thinner. Blend well.

6. Slit the tops of the pita breads and toast them lightly. Fill with the falafel, shredded lettuce, tomato, onion and cucumbers. Spoon a little yogurt on top as well, if desired.

Rosemary and Pepper Marinated Olives with Feta Cheese

Taste a bit of Greece in this delightful, versatile bowl of color, flavor and texture that includes smoky olives and bite-sized cubes of crumbly feta.

Besides imparting a sweet and pungent flavor to the dish, rosemary, a native Mediterranean herb, is also a good source of iron, calcium and vitamin B6. Rosemary helps to improve digestion and also enhances memory and concentration.

Serves 2

Ingredients:

1 cup Kalamata olives, pitted and sliced
½ cup feta cheese, diced
2 tablespoons extra virgin olive oil
1 lemon
Zest from half lemon, grated

2 cloves garlic, sliced
1 teaspoon fresh rosemary, chopped
Pinch of crushed red pepper
Salt and freshly ground pepper to taste

Method:

1. In a small mixing bowl, mix together the cheese and olives.
2. Sprinkle with the olive oil, lemon zest, garlic and rosemary. Then season with red pepper, salt and pepper to taste. Stir again. Drizzle olive oil and add lemon juice. Toss well to coat.
3. Cover and refrigerate for at least an hour before serving. For better flavor, make one day in advance. Serve with some pita bread or warm slices of French baguette.

Shallow Fried Cheesy Zucchini Balls

In Greece, zucchini balls are called '*Kolokithokeftedes.*' This low calorie snack is easy to make and the perfect way to sneak in some veggies.

In addition to the protein rich feta cheese, zucchini adds antioxidants, potassium and vitamin A to your diet, helping your body to metabolize cholesterol, preventing constipation and curbing overeating.

Serves 4

Ingredients:

2 cups zucchini, grated and squeezed
¼ cup of feta, crumbled
1 clove garlic, chopped
1 medium onions, chopped
1 tablespoon herbs (such as mint, dill and parsley), chopped

1 egg, lightly beaten
1 small carrot, grated
½ cup flour and/or breadcrumbs
3 tablespoons olive oil
Salt and pepper to taste

Method:

1. In a large bowl, mix the zucchini, onion, egg, feta, garlic and herbs. Season with salt and pepper. Mix well using your hands so that all the ingredients are well blended. Add enough flour or breadcrumbs for binding purposes if there is too much liquid.
2. Shape this mixture into 2-inch wide balls, and dust the balls in flour.
3. Heat a tablespoon of oil in a non-stick pan and fry in until golden brown. Set aside to cool. Serve hot with tomatoes or Greek yogurt.

Baked Sweet Potato Wedges with Cheese and Garlic

When you yearn for French fries, bake yourself a batch of sweet potato wedges instead. Brimming with the flavors of the Mediterranean, the sweetness of the sweet potatoes blends perfectly with the tanginess of the cheese and warmth of the oregano.

The sweet potato wedges are not just delicious and addictive but fat-free and relatively low in sodium. They are very nutritious too, as they are high in calcium, potassium, vitamins A and C, beta-carotene and fiber.

Serves 2

Ingredients:

2 medium sweet potatoes, peeled and cut into ½ inch wedges
2 tablespoons of olive oil, divided
2 cloves of garlic, finely minced

¼ teaspoon dried oregano
½ cup Parmesan cheese, grated
Salt to taste

Method:

1. Preheat oven to 450°F.
2. In a large bowl, toss sweet potato wedges with half of the olive oil, plus garlic, salt and cheese. Toss well to coat the fries.
3. Drizzle 1 tablespoon olive oil on a baking sheet, and place in oven for a few minutes. Remove pan from oven and spread out sweet potatoes wedges evenly so that none are touching.
4. Place the wedges in oven and bake for 15 minutes. Then, turn them over, and bake again until fries become slightly golden brown and begin to crisp up a bit. This should take for another 12-15 minutes.
5. Try a wedge and add more salt or cheese if desired.

Fresh Mozzarella, Cherry Tomato and Basil Sticks

This is an easy to make snack with the essential Mediterranean ingredients that supply a healthy dose of many essential vitamins and minerals.

Fragrant and flavorful, fresh basil is a popular herb in Italian cooking contains powerful antioxidants which can help protect you from cancer and heart disease.

Serves 2

Ingredients:

8 cherry tomatoes
8 small fresh mozzarella balls
8 fresh basil leaves
8 1-inch cubes crusty Italian bread

Extra virgin olive oil, to drizzle
Salt & freshly ground pepper, to taste
8 cocktail picks

Method:

1. Thread mozzarella, basil, tomatoes and a bread cube on a cocktail pick. Drizzle with oil and sprinkle with salt and pepper.

Moroccan Toasted Almonds with Cilantro

This popular snack originated in Morocco, and it beats any packaged convenience food in health and nutritional value. Most of all, it is easy to prepare and convenient to pack as a mid-day snack for a day at work.

Tasty and satiating almonds are an excellent source of vitamin E and magnesium as well as being a good source of protein and fiber.

Serves 2

Ingredients:

1 cup blanched almonds
3 tablespoons olive oil

1 teaspoon cilantro, finely ground
Salt to taste

Method:

1. Heat the oil in a small frying pan. Add the nuts in small batches and fry over medium heat until evenly crisp and brown.
2. Transfer the almonds to a bowl, and add the coriander and salt. Mix well to coat the almonds, and allow them to cool.

Spinach and Feta Cheese Toast

The Mediterranean Diet owes its popularity as much to its health benefits as it does to the simplicity of the ingredients and preparation. This delicious yet quick snack proves that health and taste does go hand in hand.

Spinach provides plenty of vitamin C, potassium, calcium and fiber, along with carotenoids and cancer-fighting indoles. Feta cheese is lower in fat and calories than most other types of cheese and is therefore a preferred ingredient in weight loss diets. It also contributes to improved metabolism and stronger bones.

Serves 2

Ingredients:

½ tablespoon olive oil
1 clove garlic, minced
¼ pound spinach
4 chunky slices brown baguette

4 tablespoons of feta cheese, crumbled
1 pinch red pepper flakes
Salt & pepper to taste

Method:

1. In a frying pan, heat the oil, and fry the garlic over medium-low heat until it begins to soften. Add the spinach. Cook until the spinach has heated and moisture has evaporated. Season with salt and pepper.
2. Toast the bread in a grill or a toaster until golden and crisp on both sides. To serve, add about 2 tablespoons of feta onto the warm toast and divide the cooked spinach equally between the two slices. Sprinkle some red pepper flakes on each, and place the remaining toasted baguette slices on top.
3. Serve warm.

Roasted Eggplant Hummus

Yes, it is true that everything tastes better when it has hummus on it, and when combined with roasted eggplant, hummus adds a lovely smoky flavor. Eggplant has a neutral flavor and a toothsome texture that is great for sauces.

Eggplants contain fiber and potassium that complements your weight-loss efforts while the skin of the vegetable contains a compound called chlorogenic acid which is known to have cancer fighting and antiviral properties.

Serves 4

Ingredients:

1 large eggplant

3 tablespoons olive oil, divided

½ cup canned chickpeas, drained

1 ½ tablespoons fresh lemon juice

2 teaspoons tahini (sesame seed paste)

1 garlic clove, minced

2 teaspoons chopped fresh parsley

Method:

1. Preheat oven to 400°F.
2. Cut eggplant in half lengthwise, prick the skin with a fork and place on a greased baking sheet. Brush with olive oil, and sprinkle some salt on the eggplant.
3. Bake for about 40 minutes or until soft and golden brown. Slice the eggplant open, and allow it to cool.
4. Discard the skin and scoop the flesh into a food processor with the chickpeas, olive oil, lemon juice, tahini, garlic and salt. Blend until the mixture is almost smooth. Add some water if the hummus is too thick. Adjust the seasonings to your taste.
5. Transfer hummus to bowl, and stir in parsley. Garnish with olive oil.
6. Serve with pita bread and some sliced cucumber on the side.

Spiced Chickpea Tidbits

Reach out for this delicious, addictive snack when you are bored or simply restless. You can make it in a jiffy or prepare it and store it for an emergency energy boosts.

Originally cultivated in the Mediterranean and the Middle East, the extremely versatile chickpeas, also known as garbanzo beans, are prized for their high protein and fiber content, and also contain several key vitamins and minerals like folate, calcium, manganese, choline, selenium, iron and zinc.

Serves 4

Ingredients:

1 15 ounce can of garbanzo beans or chickpeas, rinsed and drained

2 teaspoons ground cumin

1 teaspoon dried marjoram

¼ teaspoon ground allspice

1 tablespoon extra virgin olive oil

Salt to taste

Method:

1. Preheat oven to 450°F.

2. Dab chickpeas dry and toss in a bowl with cumin, marjoram, allspice, olive oil and salt. Spread on a baking sheet.
3. Bake for 30 to 40 minutes, stirring once or twice, until browned and crunchy. Allow to cool on the baking sheet before serving.

Beverages

Date and almond smoothie

The date and almond smoothie will keep your energy levels up for the whole morning, so it's a perfect way to start your day. This combination of almond milk and pitted dates creates a smoothie so rich and creamy, it almost resembles a milkshake.

This rich beverage has almonds as a main ingredient. Almonds are an excellent source of protein, vitamin E, copper, magnesium and bone-building calcium.

Serves 2

Ingredients:

2 cups almond milk
½ cup pitted dates
2 tablespoons cashew nuts

1 cup low-fat, plain yogurt
1 cup apple cider or apple juice
1 cup ice

Method:

1. Blend almond milk, dates, cashews, yogurt, apple cider and ice until it's nice and smooth.
2. If you think your dates are a bit dry, it would help if you soak then for around 10 minutes in warm water and drain well, before blending.

Orange, Lime and Pineapple Smoothie

Start your day off right with this refreshing orange, lime and pineapple smoothie. With plenty of healthy fruits and yogurt protein, it is also a great way to get back your energy after a workout or when you just want to eat light instead of a heavy meal.

This smoothie includes the nutrient-dense pineapple, which is high in vitamin C and the enzyme bromelain, both of which play a key role in the healing process.

Serves 2

Ingredients:

3 oranges

2 cup of pineapple chunks

2 pineapple wedges

2 mint leaves

1 lime

2 cups vanilla Greek yogurt

Some ice cubes

Method:

1. Combine the orange and pineapple with the Greek yogurt in a blender, and drop in ice cubes until you reach the desired consistency.
2. Serve in a tall smoothie glass or a hurricane glass, garnished with a pineapple wedges and a mint leaf.

Pomegranate Lemonade with Ginger Juice

They say when life gives you pomegranates, make gingery lemonade. In this delicious Mediterranean beverage, the addition of pomegranate adds a sweet but tart note, and also provides plenty of antioxidants that are beneficial for your health.

Pomegranate has anti-cancer and immune supporting effects and is a great source of vitamin C, K and dietary fiber. It helps to lower cholesterol and high blood pressure as well as reduce other cardiac risk factors.

Serves 2

Ingredients:

3 cups pomegranate seeds

2 cups water

Thick slice of ginger, peeled and crushed

Freshly squeezed juice of one lemon

Some ice cubes

Method:

1. Deseed the pomegranate.
2. Put the pomegranate seeds, lemon juice and crushed ginger into a blender, and blend for a while. Drop in ice cubes until you reach the desired consistency.
3. Pour the blended juice through a strainer to remove the pomegranate seeds and the ginger fibers.
4. Serve in martini glasses with a lemon wedge or add a splash of vodka to make this an interesting cocktail.

Almond, Cashew and Berry Smoothie

The combination of berries, nuts and Greek yogurt can never be a bad idea. This is an especially healthy indulgence.

This simple concoction results in a beverage that has incredibly healthy ingredients which include nuts that pack a high-protein punch and berries which are loaded with vitamins, anti-oxidants, minerals and phytochemicals known to reduce the risk of heart diseases and certain types of cancer.

Serves 2

Ingredients:

¼ cup of cashew nuts
½ cup of almond milk
½ cup Greek yogurt

1 cup of fresh strawberries, raspberries and blueberries
1 mint sprig

Method:

1. Blend cashew nuts, almond milk, and Greek yogurt with some ice cubes until it's nice and smooth.
2. Serve in a tall glass topped with a mint sprig and a raspberry and blueberry.

Rose and Raspberry Cooler

Dazzling red raspberries and fragrant rosewater combine to make a thirst-quenching, vividly colored cooler.

Raspberries contains high levels of many vitamins and minerals, including potassium which is required for maintaining healthy blood pressure, calcium, which is important for bone development and growth and carotenoids, lutein and zeaxanthin, which protect eyesight.

Serves 2

Ingredients:

12 fresh raspberries
2 teaspoons honey
6 drops rose water
Chilled club soda

Rose petals (edible, not treated with pesticides)
One lemon wedge, for garnish
Ice cubes

Method:

1. Blend the raspberries, honey and rosewater until smooth. Strain through a sieve. Discard the solids.

2. Pour in the soda.
3. Stir in the ice and scatter the rose petals over the top just before serving.

Fruity Tea Sangria

Your typical Spanish beverage, sangria is usually made with red wine, chopped fruit, some sweetener and often brandy. Each sip and every bite of this luscious assortment of fruit and fruit juices can be quite refreshing on a warm day. The recipe below is wine free, but if desired, substitute a red Spanish wine for the club soda.

The fruit and fruit juices in sangria pack a powerful nutritional punch. The orange juice adds plenty of vitamin C, which protects cells by neutralizing free radicals. Oranges also contain soluble fiber, which lowers cholesterol and potassium, which helps your heart to function efficiently. The citrus limonoids in oranges help fight cancer, including that of the lung, skin, stomach, breast and colon.

Serves 4

Ingredients:

1 tea bag (or1 teaspoon loose-leaf tea in an infuser)

1 cinnamon stick

1 cup boiling water

4 teaspoons sugar

1 cup freshly squeezed orange juice

2 cups pomegranate juice

1 orange, sliced

1 peach, sliced

1 lemon, sliced

1 apple, cut into ½ inch chunks

1 lime, sliced

3 cups chilled club soda

Method:

1. Steep tea bags and cinnamon stick in boiling water for 4-5 minutes. Discard tea bags, and dissolve sugar in the tea.
2. In a large pitcher or bowl, combine the cinnamon flavored tea, orange juice, pomegranate juice, orange, peach, lemon, apple and lime. Stir until well mixed.
3. Refrigerate for at least 2 hours.
4. Just before serving, stir in some club soda. Serve in glasses over ice.

Creamy Fig, Banana and Almond Smoothie

Thick, smooth and rich, this smoothie is a perfect start to a busy day. It can also reinvigorate you after a tough workout. The deliciously sweet figs make the drink chock full of calcium, and the magnesium content helps the body to absorb the calcium efficiently.

Figs also provide vitamin K which helps to create bone-forming cells that the body requires for strong, healthy bones.

Serves 4

Ingredients:

½ cup dried figs, rehydrated in water

2 bananas

3 tablespoons cacao powder

1 tablespoons almond butter

3 cups almond milk

½ tsp vanilla

2 tablespoon honey

Method:

1. Combine bananas, figs, almond butter, vanilla, cacao powder, honey and almond milk in a blender, and blend until smooth.
2. Serve immediately in a tall smoothie glass.

Spicy Pomegranate Surprise

The fresh fruit juices simmer with spices to make a fragrant, warming beverage for a special holiday dinner or gathering.

The Mediterranean region is home to a wide variety of grapes. This amazing fruit reduces the risk of heart disease by relaxing the blood vessels allowing blood to more easily flow. This is due to antioxidants called polyphenols found in the skin and seeds of grapes. One of the most important of these is resveratrol, which is known to prevent damages to blood vessels.

Serves 4

Ingredients:

4 cups pomegranate juice

4 cups white grape juice

1 cup pineapple juice

1 (1-inch-long) cinnamon stick

2 whole cloves

4 thin fresh ginger slices

Pineapple wedges, for garnish

Orange rind curls, for garnish

Method:

1. In a non-reactive saucepan, heat cinnamon stick, cloves, and ginger over medium heat, stirring constantly until the spices are fragrant.

2. Slowly stir the juices, and bring to a boil over medium-high heat. Bring down the heat to medium-low, and let simmer for 10 to 12 minutes.
3. Pour the juices through a wire-mesh strainer into a jar. Discard the solids. Serve warm.
4. Garnish with pineapple wedges and orange rind curls.

Ayran (Turkish savory yogurt drink)

After enjoying a full, spicy meal, you will need a little bit of help with your digestive process. Turkey's national drink, ayran, is a refreshing concoction which will cool your mouth after a spicy meal as well as aid with digestion.

Ayran is a good source of beneficial bacteria that is necessary for a well-functioning digestive system. Probiotics, the "good" bacteria found in many yogurts, will keep your system strong by boosting the microflora within your intestines. This improves the digestive process, removing excess gases and boosting your immune system. Ayran also supplies an abundance of calcium and vitamin D.

Serves 2

Ingredients:

2 cups plain yogurt
2 cups water

Salt to taste
6 fresh mint leaves, for garnish

Method:

1. Combine yogurt and water in blender and process until a smooth and creamy texture is reached. Add salt to taste
2. Serve chilled with fresh mint.

Healing Grapefruit Juice

Combine the sweetness of grapefruit with the spicy flavor of fennel to produce a refreshing and reinvigorating drink.

This delicious glass of grapefruit juice with the added flavor of fennel is known to fight and prevent serious health concerns like arthritis, cancer, high cholesterol and weight loss. Fennel juice has qualities that make it a useful detoxifier and an aid in digestion.

Servings 4

Ingredients:

3 large ruby red grapefruits

1 large celery stalk, sliced

Celery stalks, for garnish

1 fennel bulb with fronds

1 cup filtered water

Honey to taste

Method:

1. Clean, and thinly slice the celery. Bring water to a boil in a medium sauce pan. Once it starts boiling, add celery and return it to a boil for about 1 minute, stirring occasionally. Remove from the heat. Allow to cool to room temperature. Strain the celery syrup through a fine mesh strainer into another container. Press the celery to extract as much syrup as possible.

2. Wash the fennel well, to remove any traces of pesticides or dirt. Roughly chop it into small pieces that would fit into your juicer. Juice the fennel. Save the fennel juice in a pitcher.

3. Now, juice the grapefruits. Add the grapefruit juice and celery syrup to the pitcher containing the fennel juice. Mix well. Add water to reach the consistency you desire and honey as desired.

4. Garnish with celery stalk and serve.

Conclusion

There are three key aspects of the Mediterranean Diet which when applied sincerely to your lifestyle can bring effective weight loss benefits as well as lifelong health. These are the use of fresh ingredients, the inclusion of certain food ingredients on a daily basis and moderating the consumption of certain ingredients to once a week or once or twice a month.

Eat fresh fruits and vegetables at every meal, every day. Eat fish, seafood and legumes at least once or twice a week. Reduce meat consumption to once or twice a week.

Of course, it goes without saying that depending on the amount of physical activity that your lifestyle requires, you need to adjust these basic principles. For instance, if you partake in athletic activities or physically strenuous sports, then you may need more protein and could reasonably increase your meat consumption. This does not mean that you forego eating fresh fruits and vegetables. Consider other factors such as age and your body's ability to process the nutrients in your food.

Above all else, avoid or reduce all kinds of processed food and dairy products other than Greek yogurt and cheese. You will soon realize that eating fresh ingredients will produce better results that are readily visible in the way you look and feel. You'll see results on the scale as well.

Finally, if you enjoyed this book, then I'd like to ask you for a favor, would you be kind enough to leave a review for this book on Amazon? It'd be greatly appreciated!

Be sure to check out our website at www.thetotalevolution.com for more information.

Thank you!

Our Other Books

Below you'll find some of our other books that are popular on Amazon.com and the international sites.

Master Cleanse: How To Do A Natural Detox The Right Way And Lose Weight Fast

Mayo Clinic Diet: A Proven Diet Plan For Lifelong Weight Loss

Glycemic Index Diet: A Proven Diet Plan For Weight Loss and Healthy Eating With No Calorie Counting

Clean Eating Diet: A 10 Day Diet Plan To Eat Clean, Lose Weight And Supercharge Your Body

Wheat Belly: The Anti-Diet - A Guide To Gluten Free Eating And A Slimmer Belly

IIFYM: Flexible Dieting - Sculpt The Perfect Body While Eating The Foods You Love

The Dukan Diet: A High Protein Diet Plan To Lose Weight And Keep It Off For Life

Acid Reflux Diet: A Beginner's Guide To Natural Cures And Recipes For Acid Reflux, GERD And Heartburn

Hypothyroidism Diet: Natural Remedies & Foods To Boost Your Energy & Jump Start Your Weight Loss

It Starts With Food: A 30 Day Diet Plan To Reset Your Body, Lose Weight And Become A Healthier You

17684916R00065

Printed in Great Britain
by Amazon

THIS |
BELONGS TO:

BIRD CARE LOG

TODAY'S DATE: _____

FOOD

-
-

CLEAN WATER

-
-

PLAYTIME

-
-

HEALTH

-
-

WEEKLY CLEANING OF CAGE AND FOOD & WATER BOWLS

-
-
-
-

OTHER NOTES

_____

_____

_____

_____

_____

BIRD CARE LOG

TODAY'S DATE: _____

FOOD

-
-

CLEAN WATER

-
-

PLAYTIME

-
-

HEALTH

-
-

WEEKLY CLEANING OF CAGE AND FOOD & WATER BOWLS

-
-
-
-

OTHER NOTES

BIRD CARE LOG

Today's Date: _____

FOOD

-
-

CLEAN WATER

-
-

PLAYTIME

-
-

HEALTH

-
-

WEEKLY CLEANING OF CAGE AND FOOD & WATER BOWLS

-
-
-
-

OTHER NOTES

_____

_____

_____

_____

_____

BIRD CARE LOG

TODAY'S DATE: _____

FOOD

-
-

CLEAN WATER

-
-

PLAYTIME

-
-

HEALTH

-
-

WEEKLY CLEANING OF CAGE AND FOOD & WATER BOWLS

-
-
-
-

OTHER NOTES

_____
_____
_____
_____
_____

BIRD CARE LOG

TODAY'S DATE: _____

FOOD

-
-

CLEAN WATER

-
-

PLAYTIME

-
-

HEALTH

-
-

WEEKLY CLEANING OF CAGE AND FOOD & WATER BOWLS

-
-
-
-

OTHER NOTES

_____

_____

_____

_____

_____

BIRD CARE LOG

TODAY'S DATE: _____

FOOD

-
-

CLEAN WATER

-
-

PLAYTIME

-
-

HEALTH

-
-

WEEKLY CLEANING OF CAGE AND FOOD & WATER BOWLS

-
-
-
-

OTHER NOTES

_____
_____
_____
_____
_____

BIRD CARE LOG

TODAY'S DATE: _____

FOOD

-
-

CLEAN WATER

-
-

PLAYTIME

-
-

HEALTH

-
-

WEEKLY CLEANING OF CAGE AND FOOD & WATER BOWLS

-
-
-
-

OTHER NOTES

BIRD CARE LOG

Today's Date: _____

FOOD

-
-

CLEAN WATER

-
-

PLAYTIME

-
-

HEALTH

-
-

WEEKLY CLEANING OF CAGE AND FOOD & WATER BOWLS

-
-
-
-

OTHER NOTES

_____

_____

_____

_____

_____

BIRD CARE LOG

TODAY'S DATE: _____

FOOD

-
-

CLEAN WATER

-
-

PLAYTIME

-
-

HEALTH

-
-

WEEKLY CLEANING OF CAGE AND FOOD & WATER BOWLS

-
-
-
-

OTHER NOTES

_____
_____
_____
_____
_____

BIRD CARE LOG

TODAY'S DATE: _____

FOOD

-
-

CLEAN WATER

-
-

PLAYTIME

-
-

HEALTH

-
-

WEEKLY CLEANING OF CAGE AND FOOD & WATER BOWLS

-
-
-
-

OTHER NOTES

_____
_____
_____
_____
_____

BIRD CARE LOG

TODAY'S DATE: _____

FOOD

-
-

CLEAN WATER

-
-

PLAYTIME

-
-

HEALTH

-
-

WEEKLY CLEANING OF CAGE AND FOOD & WATER BOWLS

-
-
-
-

OTHER NOTES

BIRD CARE LOG

TODAY'S DATE: _____

FOOD

-
-

CLEAN WATER

-
-

PLAYTIME

-
-

HEALTH

-
-

WEEKLY CLEANING OF CAGE AND FOOD & WATER BOWLS

-
-
-
-

OTHER NOTES

_____
_____
_____
_____
_____

BIRD CARE LOG

TODAY'S DATE: _____

FOOD

-
-

CLEAN WATER

-
-

PLAYTIME

-
-

HEALTH

-
-

WEEKLY CLEANING OF CAGE AND FOOD & WATER BOWLS

-
-
-
-

OTHER NOTES

_____

_____

_____

_____

_____

BIRD CARE LOG

Today's Date: _____

FOOD

-
-

CLEAN WATER

-
-

PLAYTIME

-
-

HEALTH

-
-

WEEKLY CLEANING OF CAGE AND FOOD & WATER BOWLS

-
-
-
-

OTHER NOTES

_____

_____

_____

_____

_____

BIRD CARE LOG

TODAY'S DATE: _____

FOOD

-
-

CLEAN WATER

-
-

PLAYTIME

-
-

HEALTH

-
-

WEEKLY CLEANING OF CAGE AND FOOD & WATER BOWLS

-
-
-
-

OTHER NOTES

BIRD CARE LOG

TODAY'S DATE: _____

FOOD

-
-

CLEAN WATER

-
-

PLAYTIME

-
-

HEALTH

-
-

WEEKLY CLEANING OF CAGE AND FOOD & WATER BOWLS

-
-
-
-

OTHER NOTES

_____
_____
_____
_____
_____

BIRD CARE LOG

TODAY'S DATE: _____

FOOD

-
-

CLEAN WATER

-
-

PLAYTIME

-
-

HEALTH

-
-

WEEKLY CLEANING OF CAGE AND FOOD & WATER BOWLS

-
-
-
-

OTHER NOTES

_____

_____

_____

_____

_____

BIRD CARE LOG

TODAY'S DATE: _____

FOOD

-
-

CLEAN WATER

-
-

PLAYTIME

-
-

HEALTH

-
-

WEEKLY CLEANING OF CAGE AND FOOD & WATER BOWLS

-
-
-
-

OTHER NOTES

_____

_____

_____

_____

BIRD CARE LOG

Today's Date: _____

FOOD

-
-

CLEAN WATER

-
-

PLAYTIME

-
-

HEALTH

-
-

WEEKLY CLEANING OF CAGE AND FOOD & WATER BOWLS

-
-
-
-

OTHER NOTES

_____

_____

_____

_____

_____

BIRD CARE LOG

Today's Date: _____

FOOD

-
-

CLEAN WATER

-
-

PLAYTIME

-
-

HEALTH

-
-

WEEKLY CLEANING OF CAGE AND FOOD & WATER BOWLS

-
-
-
-

OTHER NOTES

_____
_____
_____
_____
_____

BIRD CARE LOG

TODAY'S DATE: _____

FOOD

-
-

CLEAN WATER

-
-

PLAYTIME

-
-

HEALTH

-
-

WEEKLY CLEANING OF CAGE AND FOOD & WATER BOWLS

-
-
-
-

OTHER NOTES

_____
_____
_____
_____
_____

BIRD CARE LOG

TODAY'S DATE: _____

FOOD

-
-

CLEAN WATER

-
-

PLAYTIME

-
-

HEALTH

-
-

WEEKLY CLEANING OF CAGE AND FOOD & WATER BOWLS

-
-
-
-

OTHER NOTES

_____

_____

_____

_____

_____

BIRD CARE LOG

TODAY'S DATE: _____

FOOD

-
-

CLEAN WATER

-
-

PLAYTIME

-
-

HEALTH

-
-

WEEKLY CLEANING OF CAGE AND FOOD & WATER BOWLS

-
-
-
-

OTHER NOTES

_____

_____

_____

_____

_____

BIRD CARE LOG

TODAY'S DATE: _____

FOOD

-
-

CLEAN WATER

-
-

PLAYTIME

-
-

HEALTH

-
-

WEEKLY CLEANING OF CAGE AND FOOD & WATER BOWLS

-
-
-
-

OTHER NOTES

_____

_____

_____

_____

_____

BIRD CARE LOG

TODAY'S DATE: _____

FOOD

-
-

CLEAN WATER

-
-

PLAYTIME

-
-

HEALTH

-
-

WEEKLY CLEANING OF CAGE AND FOOD & WATER BOWLS

-
-
-
-

OTHER NOTES

_____

_____

_____

_____

_____

_____

BIRD CARE LOG

TODAY'S DATE: _____

FOOD

-
-

CLEAN WATER

-
-

PLAYTIME

-
-

HEALTH

-
-

WEEKLY CLEANING OF CAGE AND FOOD & WATER BOWLS

-
-
-
-

OTHER NOTES

_____

_____

_____

_____

_____

BIRD CARE LOG

Today's Date: _____

FOOD

-
-

CLEAN WATER

-
-

PLAYTIME

-
-

HEALTH

-
-

WEEKLY CLEANING OF CAGE AND FOOD & WATER BOWLS

-
-
-
-

OTHER NOTES

_____

_____

_____

_____

_____

BIRD CARE LOG

TODAY'S DATE: _____

FOOD

-
-

CLEAN WATER

-
-

PLAYTIME

-
-

HEALTH

-
-

WEEKLY CLEANING OF CAGE AND FOOD & WATER BOWLS

-
-
-
-

OTHER NOTES

_____
_____
_____
_____

BIRD CARE LOG

TODAY'S DATE: _____

FOOD

-
-

CLEAN WATER

-
-

PLAYTIME

-
-

HEALTH

-
-

WEEKLY CLEANING OF CAGE AND FOOD & WATER BOWLS

-
-
-
-

OTHER NOTES

_____

_____

_____

_____

_____

BIRD CARE LOG

Today's Date: _____

FOOD

-
-

CLEAN WATER

-
-

PLAYTIME

-
-

HEALTH

-
-

WEEKLY CLEANING OF CAGE AND FOOD & WATER BOWLS

-
-
-
-

OTHER NOTES

_____

_____

_____

_____

_____

BIRD CARE LOG

TODAY'S DATE: _____

FOOD

-
-

CLEAN WATER

-
-

PLAYTIME

-
-

HEALTH

-
-

WEEKLY CLEANING OF CAGE AND FOOD & WATER BOWLS

-
-
-
-

OTHER NOTES

_____

_____

_____

_____

_____

BIRD CARE LOG

TODAY'S DATE: _____

FOOD

-
-

CLEAN WATER

-
-

PLAYTIME

-
-

HEALTH

-
-

WEEKLY CLEANING OF CAGE AND FOOD & WATER BOWLS

-
-
-
-

OTHER NOTES

BIRD CARE LOG

TODAY'S DATE: _____

FOOD

-
-

CLEAN WATER

-
-

PLAYTIME

-
-

HEALTH

-
-

WEEKLY CLEANING OF CAGE AND FOOD & WATER BOWLS

-
-
-
-

OTHER NOTES

_____

_____

_____

_____

_____

BIRD CARE LOG

Today's Date: _____

FOOD

-
-

CLEAN WATER

-
-

PLAYTIME

-
-

HEALTH

-
-

WEEKLY CLEANING OF CAGE AND FOOD & WATER BOWLS

-
-
-
-

OTHER NOTES

_____

_____

_____

_____

BIRD CARE LOG

Today's Date: _____

FOOD

-
-

CLEAN WATER

-
-

PLAYTIME

-
-

HEALTH

-
-

WEEKLY CLEANING OF CAGE AND FOOD & WATER BOWLS

-
-
-
-

OTHER NOTES

_____

_____

_____

_____

_____

BIRD CARE LOG

TODAY'S DATE: _____

FOOD

-
-

CLEAN WATER

-
-

PLAYTIME

-
-

HEALTH

-
-

WEEKLY CLEANING OF CAGE AND FOOD & WATER BOWLS

-
-
-
-

OTHER NOTES

_____

_____

_____

_____

_____

BIRD CARE LOG

TODAY'S DATE: _____

FOOD

-
-

CLEAN WATER

-
-

PLAYTIME

-
-

HEALTH

-
-

WEEKLY CLEANING OF CAGE AND FOOD & WATER BOWLS

-
-
-
-

OTHER NOTES

_____

_____

_____

_____

_____

BIRD CARE LOG

TODAY'S DATE: _____

FOOD

-
-

CLEAN WATER

-
-

PLAYTIME

-
-

HEALTH

-
-

WEEKLY CLEANING OF CAGE AND FOOD & WATER BOWLS

-
-
-
-

OTHER NOTES

BIRD CARE LOG

TODAY'S DATE: _____

FOOD

-
-

CLEAN WATER

-
-

PLAYTIME

-
-

HEALTH

-
-

WEEKLY CLEANING OF CAGE AND FOOD & WATER BOWLS

-
-
-
-

OTHER NOTES

_____

_____

_____

_____

_____

BIRD CARE LOG

TODAY'S DATE: _____

FOOD

-
-

CLEAN WATER

-
-

PLAYTIME

-
-

HEALTH

-
-

WEEKLY CLEANING OF CAGE AND FOOD & WATER BOWLS

-
-
-
-

OTHER NOTES

_____

_____

_____

_____

_____

BIRD CARE LOG

TODAY'S DATE: _____

FOOD

-
-

CLEAN WATER

-
-

PLAYTIME

-
-

HEALTH

-
-

WEEKLY CLEANING OF CAGE AND FOOD & WATER BOWLS

-
-
-
-

OTHER NOTES

_____

_____

_____

_____

_____

BIRD CARE LOG

TODAY'S DATE: _____

FOOD

-
-

CLEAN WATER

-
-

PLAYTIME

-
-

HEALTH

-
-

WEEKLY CLEANING OF CAGE AND FOOD & WATER BOWLS

-
-
-
-

OTHER NOTES

_____

_____

_____

_____

_____

BIRD CARE LOG

TODAY'S DATE: _____

FOOD

-
-

CLEAN WATER

-
-

PLAYTIME

-
-

HEALTH

-
-

WEEKLY CLEANING OF CAGE AND FOOD & WATER BOWLS

-
-
-
-

OTHER NOTES

_____

_____

_____

_____

_____

_____

BIRD CARE LOG

Today's Date: _____

FOOD

-
-

CLEAN WATER

-
-

PLAYTIME

-
-

HEALTH

-
-

WEEKLY CLEANING OF CAGE AND FOOD & WATER BOWLS

-
-
-
-

OTHER NOTES

_____
_____
_____
_____
_____

BIRD CARE LOG

TODAY'S DATE: _____

FOOD

-
-

CLEAN WATER

-
-

PLAYTIME

-
-

HEALTH

-
-

WEEKLY CLEANING OF CAGE AND FOOD & WATER BOWLS

-
-
-
-

OTHER NOTES

BIRD CARE LOG

TODAY'S DATE: _____

FOOD
-
-

CLEAN WATER
-
-

PLAYTIME
-
-

HEALTH
-
-

WEEKLY CLEANING OF CAGE AND FOOD & WATER BOWLS
-
-
-
-

OTHER NOTES
_____
_____
_____
_____

BIRD CARE LOG

TODAY'S DATE: _____

FOOD

-
-

CLEAN WATER

-
-

PLAYTIME

-
-

HEALTH

-
-

WEEKLY CLEANING OF CAGE AND FOOD & WATER BOWLS

-
-
-
-

OTHER NOTES

_____

_____

_____

_____

BIRD CARE LOG

TODAY'S DATE: _____

FOOD

-
-

CLEAN WATER

-
-

PLAYTIME

-
-

HEALTH

-
-

WEEKLY CLEANING OF CAGE AND FOOD & WATER BOWLS

-
-
-
-

OTHER NOTES

BIRD CARE LOG

TODAY'S DATE: _____

FOOD

-
-

CLEAN WATER

-
-

PLAYTIME

-
-

HEALTH

-
-

WEEKLY CLEANING OF CAGE AND FOOD & WATER BOWLS

-
-
-
-

OTHER NOTES

_____

_____

_____

_____

_____

BIRD CARE LOG

TODAY'S DATE: _____

FOOD

-
-

CLEAN WATER

-
-

PLAYTIME

-
-

HEALTH

-
-

WEEKLY CLEANING OF CAGE AND FOOD & WATER BOWLS

-
-
-
-

OTHER NOTES

_____

_____

_____

_____

_____

BIRD CARE LOG

TODAY'S DATE: _____

FOOD

-
-

CLEAN WATER

-
-

PLAYTIME

-
-

HEALTH

-
-

WEEKLY CLEANING OF CAGE AND FOOD & WATER BOWLS

-
-
-
-

OTHER NOTES

_____

_____

_____

_____

_____

BIRD CARE LOG

TODAY'S DATE: _____

FOOD

-
-

CLEAN WATER

-
-

PLAYTIME

-
-

HEALTH

-
-

WEEKLY CLEANING OF CAGE AND FOOD & WATER BOWLS

-
-
-
-

OTHER NOTES

_____

_____

_____

_____

_____

BIRD CARE LOG

TODAY'S DATE: _____

FOOD

-
-

CLEAN WATER

-
-

PLAYTIME

-
-

HEALTH

-
-

WEEKLY CLEANING OF CAGE AND FOOD & WATER BOWLS

-
-
-
-

OTHER NOTES

_____

_____

_____

_____

_____

_____

BIRD CARE LOG

TODAY'S DATE: _____

FOOD

-
-

CLEAN WATER

-
-

PLAYTIME

-
-

HEALTH

-
-

WEEKLY CLEANING OF CAGE AND FOOD & WATER BOWLS

-
-
-
-

OTHER NOTES

_____

_____

_____

_____

_____

BIRD CARE LOG

TODAY'S DATE: _____

FOOD

-
-

CLEAN WATER

-
-

PLAYTIME

-
-

HEALTH

-
-

WEEKLY CLEANING OF CAGE AND FOOD & WATER BOWLS

-
-
-
-

OTHER NOTES

BIRD CARE LOG

TODAY'S DATE: _____

FOOD

-
-

CLEAN WATER

-
-

PLAYTIME

-
-

HEALTH

-
-

WEEKLY CLEANING OF CAGE AND FOOD & WATER BOWLS

-
-
-
-

OTHER NOTES

_____
_____
_____
_____

BIRD CARE LOG

TODAY'S DATE: _____

FOOD

-
-

CLEAN WATER

-
-

PLAYTIME

-
-

HEALTH

-
-

WEEKLY CLEANING OF CAGE AND FOOD & WATER BOWLS

-
-
-
-

OTHER NOTES

_____

_____

_____

_____

_____

BIRD CARE LOG

Today's Date: _____

FOOD
-
-

CLEAN WATER
-
-

PLAYTIME
-
-

HEALTH
-
-

WEEKLY CLEANING OF CAGE AND FOOD & WATER BOWLS
-
-
-
-

OTHER NOTES
_____
_____
_____
_____
_____
_____

BIRD CARE LOG

TODAY'S DATE: _____

FOOD

-
-

CLEAN WATER

-
-

PLAYTIME

-
-

HEALTH

-
-

WEEKLY CLEANING OF CAGE AND FOOD & WATER BOWLS

-
-
-
-

OTHER NOTES

_____
_____
_____
_____
_____

BIRD CARE LOG

TODAY'S DATE: _____

FOOD

-
-

CLEAN WATER

-
-

PLAYTIME

-
-

HEALTH

-
-

WEEKLY CLEANING OF CAGE AND FOOD & WATER BOWLS

-
-
-
-

OTHER NOTES

BIRD CARE LOG

TODAY'S DATE: _____

FOOD

-
-

CLEAN WATER

-
-

PLAYTIME

-
-

HEALTH

-
-

WEEKLY CLEANING OF CAGE AND FOOD & WATER BOWLS

-
-
-
-

OTHER NOTES

_____

_____

_____

_____

_____

BIRD CARE LOG

TODAY'S DATE: _____

FOOD

-
-

CLEAN WATER

-
-

PLAYTIME

-
-

HEALTH

-
-

WEEKLY CLEANING OF CAGE AND FOOD & WATER BOWLS

-
-
-
-

OTHER NOTES

BIRD CARE LOG

TODAY'S DATE: _____

FOOD

-
-

CLEAN WATER

-
-

PLAYTIME

-
-

HEALTH

-
-

WEEKLY CLEANING OF CAGE AND FOOD & WATER BOWLS

-
-
-
-

OTHER NOTES

_____

_____

_____

_____

_____

BIRD CARE LOG

TODAY'S DATE: _____

FOOD

-
-

CLEAN WATER

-
-

PLAYTIME

-
-

HEALTH

-
-

WEEKLY CLEANING OF CAGE AND FOOD & WATER BOWLS

-
-
-
-

OTHER NOTES

_____
_____
_____
_____
_____
_____

BIRD CARE LOG

TODAY'S DATE: _____

FOOD

-
-

CLEAN WATER

-
-

PLAYTIME

-
-

HEALTH

-
-

WEEKLY CLEANING OF CAGE AND FOOD & WATER BOWLS

-
-
-
-

OTHER NOTES

_____

_____

_____

_____

_____

_____

BIRD CARE LOG

TODAY'S DATE: _____

FOOD

-
-

CLEAN WATER

-
-

PLAYTIME

-
-

HEALTH

-
-

WEEKLY CLEANING OF CAGE AND FOOD & WATER BOWLS

-
-
-
-

OTHER NOTES

BIRD CARE LOG

TODAY'S DATE: _____

FOOD

-
-

CLEAN WATER

-
-

PLAYTIME

-
-

HEALTH

-
-

WEEKLY CLEANING OF CAGE AND FOOD & WATER BOWLS

-
-
-
-

OTHER NOTES

_____
_____
_____
_____
_____

BIRD CARE LOG

TODAY'S DATE: _____

FOOD

-
-

CLEAN WATER

-
-

PLAYTIME

-
-

HEALTH

-
-

WEEKLY CLEANING OF CAGE AND FOOD & WATER BOWLS

-
-
-
-

OTHER NOTES

_____

_____

_____

_____

_____

_____

BIRD CARE LOG

TODAY'S DATE: _____

FOOD

-
-

CLEAN WATER

-
-

PLAYTIME

-
-

HEALTH

-
-

WEEKLY CLEANING OF CAGE AND FOOD & WATER BOWLS

-
-
-
-

OTHER NOTES

_____

_____

_____

_____

_____

BIRD CARE LOG

Today's Date: _____

FOOD

-
-

CLEAN WATER

-
-

PLAYTIME

-
-

HEALTH

-
-

WEEKLY CLEANING OF CAGE AND FOOD & WATER BOWLS

-
-
-
-

OTHER NOTES

_____

_____

_____

_____

BIRD CARE LOG

TODAY'S DATE: _____

FOOD

-
-

CLEAN WATER

-
-

PLAYTIME

-
-

HEALTH

-
-

WEEKLY CLEANING OF CAGE AND FOOD & WATER BOWLS

-
-
-
-

OTHER NOTES

_____

_____

_____

_____

_____

BIRD CARE LOG

TODAY'S DATE: _____

FOOD

-
-

CLEAN WATER

-
-

PLAYTIME

-
-

HEALTH

-
-

WEEKLY CLEANING OF CAGE AND FOOD & WATER BOWLS

-
-
-
-

OTHER NOTES

_____
_____
_____
_____
_____
_____

BIRD CARE LOG

TODAY'S DATE: _____

FOOD

-
-

CLEAN WATER

-
-

PLAYTIME

-
-

HEALTH

-
-

WEEKLY CLEANING OF CAGE AND FOOD & WATER BOWLS

-
-
-
-

OTHER NOTES

_____

_____

_____

_____

BIRD CARE LOG

TODAY'S DATE: _____

FOOD

-
-

CLEAN WATER

-
-

PLAYTIME

-
-

HEALTH

-
-

WEEKLY CLEANING OF CAGE AND FOOD & WATER BOWLS

-
-
-
-

OTHER NOTES

_____

_____

_____

_____

_____

BIRD CARE LOG

TODAY'S DATE: _____

FOOD

-
-

CLEAN WATER

-
-

PLAYTIME

-
-

HEALTH

-
-

WEEKLY CLEANING OF CAGE AND FOOD & WATER BOWLS

-
-
-
-

OTHER NOTES

_____

_____

_____

_____

_____

BIRD CARE LOG

TODAY'S DATE: _____

FOOD

-
-

CLEAN WATER

-
-

PLAYTIME

-
-

HEALTH

-
-

WEEKLY CLEANING OF CAGE AND FOOD & WATER BOWLS

-
-
-
-

OTHER NOTES

_____
_____
_____
_____
_____
_____

BIRD CARE LOG

TODAY'S DATE: _____

FOOD

-
-

CLEAN WATER

-
-

PLAYTIME

-
-

HEALTH

-
-

WEEKLY CLEANING OF CAGE AND FOOD & WATER BOWLS

-
-
-
-

OTHER NOTES

BIRD CARE LOG

TODAY'S DATE: _____

FOOD

-
-

CLEAN WATER

-
-

PLAYTIME

-
-

HEALTH

-
-

WEEKLY CLEANING OF CAGE AND FOOD & WATER BOWLS

-
-
-
-

OTHER NOTES

BIRD CARE LOG

TODAY'S DATE: _____

FOOD

-
-

CLEAN WATER

-
-

PLAYTIME

-
-

HEALTH

-
-

WEEKLY CLEANING OF CAGE AND FOOD & WATER BOWLS

-
-
-
-

OTHER NOTES

_____

_____

_____

_____

_____

BIRD CARE LOG

Today's Date: _____

FOOD

-
-

CLEAN WATER

-
-

PLAYTIME

-
-

HEALTH

-
-

WEEKLY CLEANING OF CAGE AND FOOD & WATER BOWLS

-
-
-
-

OTHER NOTES

_____
_____
_____
_____
_____

BIRD CARE LOG

TODAY'S DATE: _____

FOOD

-
-

CLEAN WATER

-
-

PLAYTIME

-
-

HEALTH

-
-

WEEKLY CLEANING OF CAGE AND FOOD & WATER BOWLS

-
-
-
-

OTHER NOTES

_____

_____

_____

_____

_____

BIRD CARE LOG

TODAY'S DATE: _____

FOOD

-
-

CLEAN WATER

-
-

PLAYTIME

-
-

HEALTH

-
-

WEEKLY CLEANING OF CAGE AND FOOD & WATER BOWLS

-
-
-
-

OTHER NOTES

_____

_____

_____

_____

_____

BIRD CARE LOG

Today's Date: _____

FOOD

-
-

CLEAN WATER

-
-

PLAYTIME

-
-

HEALTH

-
-

WEEKLY CLEANING OF CAGE AND FOOD & WATER BOWLS

-
-
-
-

OTHER NOTES

_____

_____

_____

_____

_____

_____

BIRD CARE LOG

TODAY'S DATE: _____

FOOD

-
-

CLEAN WATER

-
-

PLAYTIME

-
-

HEALTH

-
-

WEEKLY CLEANING OF CAGE AND FOOD & WATER BOWLS

-
-
-
-

OTHER NOTES

_____
_____
_____
_____
_____

BIRD CARE LOG

TODAY'S DATE: _____

FOOD

-
-

CLEAN WATER

-
-

PLAYTIME

-
-

HEALTH

-
-

WEEKLY CLEANING OF CAGE AND FOOD & WATER BOWLS

-
-
-
-

OTHER NOTES

_____

_____

_____

_____

_____

BIRD CARE LOG

TODAY'S DATE: _____

FOOD

-
-

CLEAN WATER

-
-

PLAYTIME

-
-

HEALTH

-
-

WEEKLY CLEANING OF CAGE AND FOOD & WATER BOWLS

-
-
-
-

OTHER NOTES

_____

_____

_____

_____

BIRD CARE LOG

TODAY'S DATE: _____

FOOD

-
-

CLEAN WATER

-
-

PLAYTIME

-
-

HEALTH

-
-

WEEKLY CLEANING OF CAGE AND FOOD & WATER BOWLS

-
-
-
-

OTHER NOTES

_____

_____

_____

_____

_____

BIRD CARE LOG

Today's Date: _____

FOOD

- •
- •

CLEAN WATER

- •
- •

PLAYTIME

- •
- •

HEALTH

- •
- •

WEEKLY CLEANING OF CAGE AND FOOD & WATER BOWLS

- •
- •
- •
- •

OTHER NOTES

_____

_____

_____

_____

BIRD CARE LOG

TODAY'S DATE: _____

FOOD

-
-

CLEAN WATER

-
-

PLAYTIME

-
-

HEALTH

-
-

WEEKLY CLEANING OF CAGE AND FOOD & WATER BOWLS

-
-
-
-

OTHER NOTES

_____

_____

_____

_____

_____

BIRD CARE LOG

TODAY'S DATE: _____

FOOD

-
-

CLEAN WATER

-
-

PLAYTIME

-
-

HEALTH

-
-

WEEKLY CLEANING OF CAGE AND FOOD & WATER BOWLS

-
-
-
-

OTHER NOTES

_____

_____

_____

_____

BIRD CARE LOG

TODAY'S DATE: _____

FOOD

-
-

CLEAN WATER

-
-

PLAYTIME

-
-

HEALTH

-
-

WEEKLY CLEANING OF CAGE AND FOOD & WATER BOWLS

-
-
-
-

OTHER NOTES

BIRD CARE LOG

TODAY'S DATE: _____

FOOD

-
-

CLEAN WATER

-
-

PLAYTIME

-
-

HEALTH

-
-

WEEKLY CLEANING OF CAGE AND FOOD & WATER BOWLS

-
-
-
-

OTHER NOTES

_____

_____

_____

_____

BIRD CARE LOG

TODAY'S DATE: _____

FOOD

-
-

CLEAN WATER

-
-

PLAYTIME

-
-

HEALTH

-
-

WEEKLY CLEANING OF CAGE AND FOOD & WATER BOWLS

-
-
-
-

OTHER NOTES

BIRD CARE LOG

TODAY'S DATE: _____

FOOD

-
-

CLEAN WATER

-
-

PLAYTIME

-
-

HEALTH

-
-

WEEKLY CLEANING OF CAGE AND FOOD & WATER BOWLS

-
-
-
-

OTHER NOTES

_____

_____

_____

_____

BIRD CARE LOG

Today's Date: _____

FOOD

-
-

CLEAN WATER

-
-

PLAYTIME

-
-

HEALTH

-
-

WEEKLY CLEANING OF CAGE AND FOOD & WATER BOWLS

-
-
-
-

OTHER NOTES

_____
_____
_____
_____
_____
_____

BIRD CARE LOG

TODAY'S DATE: _____

FOOD

-
-

CLEAN WATER

-
-

PLAYTIME

-
-

HEALTH

-
-

WEEKLY CLEANING OF CAGE AND FOOD & WATER BOWLS

-
-
-
-

OTHER NOTES

_____

_____

_____

_____

_____

_____

BIRD CARE LOG

TODAY'S DATE: _____

FOOD

-
-

CLEAN WATER

-
-

PLAYTIME

-
-

HEALTH

-
-

WEEKLY CLEANING OF CAGE AND FOOD & WATER BOWLS

-
-
-
-

OTHER NOTES

_____
_____
_____
_____
_____
_____

BIRD CARE LOG

TODAY'S DATE: _____

FOOD

-
-

CLEAN WATER

-
-

PLAYTIME

-
-

HEALTH

-
-

WEEKLY CLEANING OF CAGE AND FOOD & WATER BOWLS

-
-
-
-

OTHER NOTES

_____

_____

_____

_____

_____

BIRD CARE LOG

TODAY'S DATE: _____

FOOD

-
-

CLEAN WATER

-
-

PLAYTIME

-
-

HEALTH

-
-

WEEKLY CLEANING OF CAGE AND FOOD & WATER BOWLS

-
-
-
-

OTHER NOTES

BIRD CARE LOG

TODAY'S DATE: _____

FOOD

-
-

CLEAN WATER

-
-

PLAYTIME

-
-

HEALTH

-
-

WEEKLY CLEANING OF CAGE AND FOOD & WATER BOWLS

-
-
-
-

OTHER NOTES

_____

_____

_____

_____

_____

BIRD CARE LOG

TODAY'S DATE: _____

FOOD

-
-

CLEAN WATER

-
-

PLAYTIME

-
-

HEALTH

-
-

WEEKLY CLEANING OF CAGE AND FOOD & WATER BOWLS

-
-
-
-

OTHER NOTES

_____

_____

_____

_____

_____

BIRD CARE LOG

Today's Date: _____

FOOD

-
-

CLEAN WATER

-
-

PLAYTIME

-
-

HEALTH

-
-

WEEKLY CLEANING OF CAGE AND FOOD & WATER BOWLS

-
-
-
-

OTHER NOTES

_____

_____

_____

_____

_____

BIRD CARE LOG

TODAY'S DATE: _____

FOOD

-
-

CLEAN WATER

-
-

PLAYTIME

-
-

HEALTH

-
-

WEEKLY CLEANING OF CAGE AND FOOD & WATER BOWLS

-
-
-
-

OTHER NOTES

BIRD CARE LOG

TODAY'S DATE: _____

FOOD

-
-

CLEAN WATER

-
-

PLAYTIME

-
-

HEALTH

-
-

WEEKLY CLEANING OF CAGE AND FOOD & WATER BOWLS

-
-
-
-

OTHER NOTES

_____
_____
_____
_____

BIRD CARE LOG

TODAY'S DATE: _____

FOOD

-
-

CLEAN WATER

-
-

PLAYTIME

-
-

HEALTH

-
-

WEEKLY CLEANING OF CAGE AND FOOD & WATER BOWLS

-
-
-
-

OTHER NOTES

_____

_____

_____

_____

_____

BIRD CARE LOG

TODAY'S DATE: _____

FOOD

-
-

CLEAN WATER

-
-

PLAYTIME

-
-

HEALTH

-
-

WEEKLY CLEANING OF CAGE AND FOOD & WATER BOWLS

-
-
-
-

OTHER NOTES

_____

_____

_____

_____

_____

BIRD CARE LOG

TODAY'S DATE: _____

FOOD

-
-

CLEAN WATER

-
-

PLAYTIME

-
-

HEALTH

-
-

WEEKLY CLEANING OF CAGE AND FOOD & WATER BOWLS

-
-
-
-

OTHER NOTES

BIRD CARE LOG

TODAY'S DATE: _____

FOOD

-
-

CLEAN WATER

-
-

PLAYTIME

-
-

HEALTH

-
-

WEEKLY CLEANING OF CAGE AND FOOD & WATER BOWLS

-
-
-
-

OTHER NOTES

_____

_____

_____

_____

_____

BIRD CARE LOG

TODAY'S DATE: _____

FOOD

-
-

CLEAN WATER

-
-

PLAYTIME

-
-

HEALTH

-
-

WEEKLY CLEANING OF CAGE AND FOOD & WATER BOWLS

-
-
-
-

OTHER NOTES

_____

_____

_____

_____

_____

BIRD CARE LOG

TODAY'S DATE: _____

FOOD

-
-

CLEAN WATER

-
-

PLAYTIME

-
-

HEALTH

-
-

WEEKLY CLEANING OF CAGE AND FOOD & WATER BOWLS

-
-
-
-

OTHER NOTES

_____

_____

_____

_____

_____

_____

BIRD CARE LOG

TODAY'S DATE: _____

FOOD

-
-

CLEAN WATER

-
-

PLAYTIME

-
-

HEALTH

-
-

WEEKLY CLEANING OF CAGE AND FOOD & WATER BOWLS

-
-
-
-

OTHER NOTES

_____
_____
_____
_____
_____

BIRD CARE LOG

TODAY'S DATE: _____

FOOD

-
-

CLEAN WATER

-
-

PLAYTIME

-
-

HEALTH

-
-

WEEKLY CLEANING OF CAGE AND FOOD & WATER BOWLS

-
-
-
-

OTHER NOTES

_____
_____
_____
_____
_____

BIRD CARE LOG

TODAY'S DATE: _____

FOOD

-
-

CLEAN WATER

-
-

PLAYTIME

-
-

HEALTH

-
-

WEEKLY CLEANING OF CAGE AND FOOD & WATER BOWLS

-
-
-
-

OTHER NOTES

_____

_____

_____

_____

_____

BIRD CARE LOG

TODAY'S DATE: _____

FOOD

-
-

CLEAN WATER

-
-

PLAYTIME

-
-

HEALTH

-
-

WEEKLY CLEANING OF CAGE AND FOOD & WATER BOWLS

-
-
-
-

OTHER NOTES

BIRD CARE LOG

Today's Date: _____

FOOD

-
-

CLEAN WATER

-
-

PLAYTIME

-
-

HEALTH

-
-

WEEKLY CLEANING OF CAGE AND FOOD & WATER BOWLS

-
-
-
-

OTHER NOTES

BIRD CARE LOG

TODAY'S DATE: _____

FOOD

-
-

CLEAN WATER

-
-

PLAYTIME

-
-

HEALTH

-
-

WEEKLY CLEANING OF CAGE AND FOOD & WATER BOWLS

-
-
-
-

OTHER NOTES

BIRD CARE LOG

TODAY'S DATE: _____

FOOD

-
-

CLEAN WATER

-
-

PLAYTIME

-
-

HEALTH

-
-

WEEKLY CLEANING OF CAGE AND FOOD & WATER BOWLS

-
-
-
-

OTHER NOTES

_____
_____
_____
_____
_____

Printed in Great Britain
by Amazon